酒店情境英语(上)

Practical Hotel English & Knowledge

主　编　王向宁
编　委　胡特赐　魏　力　付媛媛　张艳妍
　　　　张　萍　姚天洋　伍秋子　崔新会
主　审　〔美〕Leo (Liu Zhigang)　〔美〕David Goodsell

图书在版编目(CIP)数据

酒店情境英语.上/王向宁主编.—北京：北京大学出版社，2014.8
(21世纪旅游英语系列教材)
ISBN 978-7-301-24644-3

Ⅰ.①酒… Ⅱ.①王… Ⅲ.①饭店—英语—高等学校—教材 Ⅳ.①H31

中国版本图书馆CIP数据核字(2014)第185264号

书　　　　名：	酒店情境英语（上）
著作责任者：	王向宁　主编
责 任 编 辑：	刘　爽
标 准 书 号：	ISBN 978-7-301-24644-3/H·3558
出 版 发 行：	北京大学出版社
地　　　　址：	北京市海淀区成府路205号　100871
网　　　　址：	http://www.pup.cn　新浪官方微博:@北京大学出版社
电 子 邮 箱：	编辑部 pupwaiwen@pup.cn　总编室 zpup@pup.cn
电　　　　话：	邮购部 62752015　发行部 62750672　编辑部 62759634　出版部 62754962
印 　刷 　者：	三河市博文印刷有限公司
经 　销 　者：	新华书店
	787毫米×980毫米　16开本　10.75印张　300千字
	2014年8月第1版　2024年1月第5次印刷
定　　　　价：	32.00元

未经许可，不得以任何方式复制或抄袭本书之部分或全部内容。
版权所有，侵权必究
举报电话：010-62752024　电子邮箱：fd@pup.cn

ACKNOWLEDGEMENTS

The aim of this textbook is to introduce Hotel English and professional knowledge and skills to Chinese readers and students. We are indebted to many sources for the passages and pictures selected for reading. With regard to the issue of copyright, we have made extensive efforts to contact the publishers and authors of these passages and pictures, but for various reasons we have been unable to establish communication in some cases. In these cases we apologize to the publishers and authors in advance and will be happy to make fuller acknowledgement in due course. For any questions concerning copyright and permissions, please contact:

E-mail: willarr@126.com

We will be happy to make any necessary arrangements for the appropriate settlement of any possible copyright issues.

前 言

《酒店情境英语》是北京市教委高校教育教学改革促进项目的成果之一,是面向全国高等院校旅游专业、酒店管理专业、英语专业(旅游、酒店、商务方向)编写的专业英语类教材,同时也可供旅游、酒店行业从业人员作为自学教材和参考书。

本教材明显有别于目前市场上的同类教材。首先,它在内容的选取上颇具特色和创新性,涵盖面客(员工与客人的交流)、面内(内部员工及上、下级的沟通)两个方面。其次,在编排上围绕不同部门的多种实际情境展开,选材上注意典型性和代表性,既强调特点和实用,又详略得当,以期学生可以触类旁通,达到举一反三的学习效果。第三,注重真实和实用性。其中涉及的对话交流部分,无论是面客还是面内,都是作者在实际工作中采录并经过提炼的。第四,版面活泼,提供真实情境图片、常用表格、实用文体等,直观易学。第五,每个单元涉猎广泛,从多元、多角度提供真实的对话交流、岗位及职责、语言训练、专业知识补充等,课文与练习相辅相成,浑然一体。

本教材的作者充分利用了所在酒店管理学院得天独厚的优质资源优势,在编写过程中,既咨询了大批来自国内外酒店业界人员,也听取了学院每年分散在全国各地四、五星级酒店实习学生的反馈,另一方面,大部分作者均有在酒店顶岗工作的经验。

本教材分上、下两册,共31个单元,内容涵盖酒店所有职能部门,既包括直接对客服务的一线部门:前厅部、客房部、餐饮部、康乐部;又包括负责酒店日常管理及安全的二线部门:人力资源部、安保部、销售部、财务部等。从语言运用角度来讲,本书内容既包括酒店员工对客服务日常用语,又包括酒店员工之间的内部交流用语。教材每个单元由以下8个模块构成:1)Lead-in Activity:通过提问制造悬念,引发学生的好奇心和求知欲;2)Job Description:描述相应工作岗位主要职责;3)Conversation:提供对客服务的日常用语、酒店员工内部交流用语;4)Useful Words and Expressions:补充在对话当中无法涉及的酒店常用语;5)Practical Form:列出酒店常用工作表格、单据及简单公文写作;6)Abbreviations and Technical Terms:介绍酒店工作中常用缩略语或者术语;7)Knowledge:提供实用的酒店知识,扩充学生知识面;8)Exercises:与正文内容相互补充,巩固学生的语言技能和专业知识。

酒店情境英语（上）

本教材在编写过程中承蒙中瑞酒店管理学院实训基地九十余家酒店相关人员的帮助，承蒙瑞士洛桑酒店管理学院咨询顾问 Alexia, Chen Weicheng, Linda 等的指导，承蒙迪拜卓美亚酒店管理学院 John Fong 的帮助，承蒙本院实习学生的协助，承蒙 David Goodsell, Leo (Liu Zhigang), Dan Garst 在语言上的把关，承蒙中瑞酒店管理学院科研管理中心在配套资金上的鼎力支持，在此表示衷心感谢！

本教材由北京第二外国语学院中瑞酒店管理学院教授王向宁担任主编，参与编写人员为胡特赐、魏力、付媛媛、张艳妍、张萍、姚天洋、伍秋子、崔新会。

鉴于时间仓促、编者水平有限，本教材难免有疏漏、不足之处，欢迎广大读者批评指正。

王向宁

2014年5月

目 录
Contents

Front Office 前厅

Unit 1 Room Reservation 客房预订 ································· 1
- Lead-in Activity 导入 ························· 1
- Job Description 岗位职责 ························· 2
- Conversation 情境对话 ························· 2
- Useful Words and Expressions 实用词汇和表达 ············· 4
- Practical Form 常用表单 ························· 5
- Abbreviations and Technical Terms 缩略语和术语 ············· 6
- Knowledge 实用小知识 ························· 7
- Exercises 练习 ························· 8

Unit 2 Guest Check-in 客人入住 ································· 10
- Lead-in Activity 导入 ························· 10
- Job Description 岗位职责 ························· 11
- Conversation 情境对话 ························· 11
- Useful Words and Expressions 实用词汇和表达 ············· 13
- Practical Form 常用表单 ························· 14
- Abbreviations and Technical Terms 缩略语和术语 ············· 16
- Knowledge 实用小知识 ························· 16
- Exercises 练习 ························· 17

Unit 3 Concierge Service 礼宾服务 ································· 19
- Lead-in Activity 导入 ························· 19
- Job Description 岗位职责 ························· 20
- Conversation 情境对话 ························· 20
- Useful Words and Expressions 实用词汇与表达 ············· 22
- Practical Form 实用表单 ························· 23
- Abbreviations and Technical Terms 缩略语和术语 ············· 24
- Knowledge 实用小知识 ························· 25

- Exercises 练习 ··· 26

Unit 4　Telephone Service 电话服务　28
- Lead-in Activity 导入 ·· 28
- Job Description 岗位职责 ··· 29
- Conversation 情境对话 ·· 29
- Useful Words and Expressions 实用词汇与表达 ······························ 31
- Practical Form 实用表单 ·· 32
- Abbreviations and Technical Terms 缩略语和术语 ························· 33
- Knowledge 实用小知识 ·· 34
- Exercises 练习 ··· 35

Unit 5　Business Center 商务中心　37
- Lead-in Activity 导入 ·· 37
- Job Description 岗位职责 ··· 38
- Conversation 情境对话 ·· 38
- Useful Words and Expressions 实用词汇与表达 ······························ 40
- Practical Form 实用表单 ·· 41
- Abbreviations and Technical Terms 缩略语和术语 ························· 42
- Knowledge 实用小知识 ·· 43
- Exercises 练习 ··· 44

Unit 6　Settling Complaints 处理投诉　46
- Lead-in Activity 导入 ·· 46
- Job Description 岗位职责 ··· 47
- Conversation 情境对话 ·· 47
- Useful Words and Expressions 实用词汇与表达 ······························ 49
- Practical Form 实用表单 ·· 50
- Abbreviations and Technical Terms 缩略语和术语 ························· 52
- Knowledge 实用小知识 ·· 52
- Exercises 练习 ··· 53

Unit 7　Guest Check-out 客人离店　55
- Lead-in Activity 导入 ·· 55

- Job Description 岗位职责 ································· 56
- Conversation 情境对话 ··································· 56
- Useful Words and Expressions 实用词汇与表达 ········· 58
- Practical Form 实用表单 ································· 59
- Abbreviations and Technical Terms 缩略语和术语 ······ 61
- Knowledge 实用小知识 ·································· 61
- Exercises 练习 ·· 62

Housekeeping 房务

Unit 8 Chamber Service 客房清理 ························· 64
- Lead-in Activity 导入 ··································· 64
- Job Description 岗位职责 ································· 65
- Conversation 情境对话 ··································· 65
- Useful Words and Expressions 实用词汇与表达 ········· 68
- Practical Form 实用表单 ································· 69
- Abbreviations and Technical Terms 缩略语和术语 ······ 70
- Knowledge 实用小知识 ·································· 71
- Exercises 练习 ·· 73

Unit 9 Laundry Service 洗衣服务 ························· 75
- Lead-in Activity 导入 ··································· 75
- Job Description 岗位职责 ································· 76
- Conversation 情境对话 ··································· 76
- Useful Words and Expressions 实用词汇与表达 ········· 79
- Practical Form 实用表单 ································· 80
- Abbreviations and Technical Terms 缩略语和术语 ······ 82
- Knowledge 实用小知识 ·································· 82
- Exercises 练习 ·· 83

Unit 10 Maintenance Service 维修保养 ···················· 85
- Lead-in Activity 导入 ··································· 85
- Job Description 岗位职责 ································· 86
- Conversation 情境对话 ··································· 86
- Useful Words and Expressions 实用词汇与表达 ········· 88

- Practical Form 实用表单 …… 89
- Abbreviations and Technical Terms 缩略语和术语 …… 91
- Knowledge 实用小知识 …… 92
- Exercises 练习 …… 92

Unit 11　Special Service 特殊服务 …… 95
- Lead-in Activity 导入 …… 95
- Job Description 岗位职责 …… 96
- Conversation 情境对话 …… 96
- Useful Words and Expressions 实用词汇与表达 …… 98
- Practical Form 实用表单 …… 99
- Abbreviations and Technical Terms 缩略语和术语 …… 101
- Knowledge 实用小知识 …… 102
- Exercises 练习 …… 102

Unit 12　Communicating with Staff 员工交流 …… 105
- Lead-in Activity 导入 …… 105
- Job Description 岗位职责 …… 106
- Conversation 情境对话 …… 106
- Useful Words and Expressions 实用词汇与表达 …… 108
- Practical Form 实用表单 …… 109
- Abbreviations and Technical Terms 缩略语和术语 …… 110
- Knowledge 实用小知识 …… 111
- Exercises 练习 …… 112

Food and Beverage (I) 餐饮（一）

Unit 13　Reservation and Seating Guests 预订与领位 …… 114
- Lead-in Activity 导入 …… 114
- Job Description 岗位职责 …… 115
- Conversation 情境对话 …… 115
- Useful Words and Expressions 实用词汇与表达 …… 117
- Practical Form 实用表单 …… 118
- Abbreviations and Technical Terms 缩略语和术语 …… 120
- Knowledge 实用小知识 …… 120

- Exercises 练习 ·········· 121

Unit 14 Taking Orders 点餐 ·········· 123
- Lead-in Activity 导入 ·········· 123
- Job Description 岗位职责 ·········· 124
- Conversation 情境对话 ·········· 124
- Useful Words and Expressions 实用词汇与表达 ·········· 127
- Practical Form 实用表单 ·········· 128
- Abbreviations and Technical Terms 缩略语和术语 ·········· 130
- Knowledge 实用小知识 ·········· 130
- Exercises 练习 ·········· 131

Unit 15 Serving Dishes 上菜 ·········· 133
- Lead-in Activity 导入 ·········· 133
- Job Description 岗位职责 ·········· 134
- Conversation 情境对话 ·········· 134
- Useful Words and Expressions 实用词汇与表达 ·········· 136
- Practical Form 实用表单 ·········· 137
- Abbreviations and Technical Terms 缩略语和术语 ·········· 139
- Knowledge 实用小知识 ·········· 139
- Exercises 练习 ·········· 140

Unit 16 Room Service 客房送餐 ·········· 142
- Lead-in Activity 导入 ·········· 142
- Job Description 岗位职责 ·········· 143
- Conversation 情境对话 ·········· 143
- Useful Words and Expressions 实用词汇与表达 ·········· 145
- Practical Form 实用表单 ·········· 146
- Abbreviations and Technical Terms 缩略语和术语 ·········· 148
- Knowledge 实用小知识 ·········· 148
- Exercises 练习 ·········· 149

练习参考答案 ·········· 151
参考书目 ·········· 158

Unit 1 Room Reservation

Lead-in Activity

Look at the pictures and discuss the questions.

- What is a reservationist?
- What does he or she do everyday?
- Would you like to be a reservationist?

酒店情境英语（上）

Job Description

▶▶ Reservationist

- Book, change, or cancel reservations;
- Be familiar with the opera system and phone system;
- Verify customer information and payment options;
- Answer inquiries of room rates, outlets and room locations;
- Handle all guests' special requests.

Conversation

Conversation 1

Taking a Reservation

(Scene: John is making a reservation at the Reservation Center through a long-distance call.)
(A= Amanda, Reservationist; J=John, Guest)

A: ABC Hotel. Reservation Centre. Amanda speaking. How may I help you?

J: Hi, I'd like to book a room during the international conference.

A: Sure. What type of room would you like?

J: I'd like a single room. How much is it for a night?

A: It's 1200 *yuan* per night.

J: Ok. I'll take it. Is breakfast included?

A: Yes, a buffet breakfast is served on the 3rd floor.

J: Great. Please hold the room for me.

A: Certainly. May I have your name, please?

J: Yes. John Smith.

New Words

reservation *n.* 预订
conference *n.* 会议，会谈
buffet *n.* 自助餐

◆ Unit 1 Room Reservation

A: Ok. Mr. Smith, I'll also need your credit card number and expiration date.

J: Fine. The credit card number is 3728 024906 54259, and the expiration date is 02/24.

A: Right. I've made the reservation. We look forward to your coming.

J: Thank you for all your help.

credit *n.* 信用,荣誉
expiration *n.* 终止,期满

Conversation 2

Confirming a Reservation

(Scene: Amanda is confirming a reservation with Tom at the Reservation Center.)
(T=Tom, Guest from a travel agency; A= Amanda, Reservationist)

A: ABC Hotel. Reservation Centre. Amanda Speaking. How may I help you?

T: Hi, Amanda. This is Tom from Sunshine Travel Agency. I am calling to confirm our reservation.

A: Hi, Tom. Which booking is that, please?

T: It's the group reservation for May 5th to 10th.

A: One moment, please. That's 20 double rooms, sea view rooms.

T: That's correct. And don't forget the rooms should be adjoining ones.

A: Ok. We've blocked off the 18th floor.

T: That's great. What are the charges again?

A: For a double room, it's 1500 *yuan* per day. We offer a 10% discount for group reservation.

T: Great. Can you confirm my reservation now?

A: OK, I'll have the confirmation number in a moment.

T: Good.

A: It's confirmed. The confirmation number is T2391, T for Tom.

T: Thank you, Amanda.

A: You're welcome, Tom. Look forward to seeing you.

New Words
confirm *v.* 证实,确定
adjoining *adj.* 毗邻的
block off 封锁,封闭
charge *n.* 费用
discount *n.* 折扣

酒店情境英语（上）

Conversation 3

Canceling a Reservation

(Scene: Amanda is receiving a phone call from Mrs. Scott who wants to cancel a reservation.)
(S= Mrs. Scott, Guest; A= Amanda, Reservationist)

A: Hello. Is that the Reservation Desk?
A: Yes, it is. This is Amanda. How can I help you?
S: Oh, hi, Amanda. This is Mrs. Scott. I made a reservation in your hotel last week.
A: Mrs. Scott, just a moment please. Yes, it is for four nights, from the 14th to 18th.
S: That's right. I'm very sorry, but I want to have a cancel.
A: That's fine. Would you like to modify it?
S: No. You see, my husband couldn't be with me because of his business trip.
A: I am sorry to hear that.
S: So I've decided to postpone my trip.
A: I understand. I've cancelled your reservation, Mrs. Scott.
S: Thank you, but will there be a cancellation charge?
A: No, because you're canceling more than 48 hours before the date.
S: Thank you so much. I'll keep your hotel in mind.

New Words
cancel v. 取消，作废
modify v. 修改
business trip 商务旅行
postpone v. 延期，推迟

Useful Words and Expressions

outlet 出口
opera system 预订系统
payment option 支付方式
room rate 房价
room location 房间位置
free parking 免费停车
high season 旺季

How long will you be staying? 您会在这儿住多久？
Let me check. 我来核对一下。
We have a vacancy. 我们有空房。
There are no rooms left. 我们已经没有空房了。
We are sorry to inform you that... 很抱歉通知您……
We look forward to serving you. 我们期待为您服务。
We are completely full now. 我们的房间都已经预订满了。

low season 淡季
half board plan 半食宿
full board plan 全食宿

I'd prefer a view of the city. 我想要一个观景房。
I'd rather be on the top floor. 我更想住在最高层。
I want a non-smoking floor. 我想住在无烟楼层。

Practical Form

Reservation Form 预订表

GUEST: 客人:
Name: 姓名: Mr./Mrs/Ms. 先生/太太/小姐
Address: 地址:
Telephone: 电话号码:
RESERVATION: 预订:
Arrival Date: 抵店日期: Departure Date: 离店日期:
No. of Nights: 拟住天数: No. of Rooms: 拟住房间数: No. of Adults: 拟住成人数:
No. of Children (under 12 years): 拟住小孩数(12岁以下):
ROOM TYPE: 房型:
■ Single 单人间
■ Double 双人间
■ Family 家庭房
■ Executive Suite 行政套房
■ Presidential Suite 总统套房
Rate: 房费: Remarks: 备注:
MEAL PLAN: 订餐计划:
■ European Plan (room only) 欧式配套(只供住房)
■ Continental Plan (bed & breakfast) 大陆式配套(住房+欧陆式早餐)
■ Modified American Plan (half board) 简易美式配套(住房+美式早餐+晚餐)
■ American Plan (3 meals) 美式配套(住房+美式早餐+午餐+晚餐)
ADDITIONAL DETAILS: 其他信息:
Confirmed: 已确认预订   Yes 是   No 否
Reservation Clerk: 预订员   Date: 日期

酒店情境英语（上）

Confirmation Mail 确认函

Mr. Tom Wilson
Sunshine Travel Agency
24 Park Lane, New York, CA 94112

Dear Mr. Wilson,

We are pleased to confirm your reservation for May 5—10.

Your confirmation number is: T2391.

Your reservation details are as follows:
- Room type: 20 double rooms (adjoining ones)
- Total stay: 5 nights
- Meal plan: MAP (half board)
- Rate: 1500 *yuan* per night (10% discount for group reservation)
- Special requests: fresh flowers in rooms, parking, early check-in

Thank you for choosing the ABC Hotel.

Sincerely,

_____

Alice Wong
Reservation Supervisor

Abbreviations and Technical Terms

ADR: Average Daily Rate 日平均房价	**CRS:** Central Reservation System 中央预订系统
EA: Expected Arrival 预计到店	**ETA:** Estimated Time of Arrival 预计到店时间
ED: Expected Departure 预计离店	**ETD:** Estimated Time of Departure 预计离店时间
FO: Front Office 前厅部	**FOM:** Front Office Manager 前厅部经理
GRP: Group 团体	**HF:** High Floor 高层
LF: Low Floor 低层	**RES:** Reservation 预订
RM: Room 房间	**R/N:** Room/Night 间夜
RR: Room Rate 房费	**RSVN:** Reservation 预订部
T/A: Travel Agent 旅行社	**VCRO:** Virtual Central Reservation Office 预订中心的预订系统

Unit 1 Room Reservation

Knowledge

Types of Room Reservation

- Advance reservation
- Confirmed reservation
- Guaranteed reservation
- Waiting reservation

Making a Hotel Reservation Online

The Reservation Department is always the guests' first contact with the hotel because many hotel guests make reservations before they start their trips. Requests for reservations are received at the hotel in different ways. But nowadays, making a hotel reservation online takes the lead. It makes the reservation process simpler and more efficient.

If you elect to make a room reservation through the Internet and do not have an established user profile, you will need to furnish

- your name
- telephone number
- billing address
- credit card type, number and expiration date
- dates of your stay
- number of rooms you will require
- number of adults and children in your party

Once you have completed and submitted the online reservation form, the information included will then be automatically sent to the Reservation System of the hotel.

Exercises

Speaking Practice

Activity 1: Discussion

Do you think you are qualified to work at the Reservation Center? Write down your strengths and weaknesses and then discuss with your partners.

Activity 2: Role-play

Role-play 1

Guest: You are Mr. Lee and want to book a double room for you and your wife from May 5th to 8th.

Clerk: You are the reservationist. Tell Mr. Lee that the room rate is 1200 *yuan* per day with breakfast. Ask Mr. Lee questions regarding the date of arrival and departure.

Role-play 2

Guest: You have booked an executive suite for your manager in the hotel for three nights. Now you have to cancel the reservation because your manager has other plans.

Clerk: You are the reservationist. You answer the call and accept the cancellation in a polite way.

Listening and Writing

Activity 1: Blank Filling—Dealing with a Cancellation

Listen and fill in the blanks.

T: Hello, is that the Reservation Desk?
A: Yes, this is Alice. How can I help you?
T: Alice, this is Terry. I am afraid I've got some bad news.
A: May I know what happened?
T: _____. All flights from New York City have been cancelled.
A: Oh, that's too bad. What are you going to do?
T: I have no idea. It _____ the weather here. Can you keep the room blocked for me?
A: Certainly, sir. Your reservation is a guaranteed one.

T: Great. Can you notify the hotel _____ of the change?
A: Definitely. Please inform us when the plane _____. So we can pick you up at the airport.
T: Ok. I will.
A: One more thing, Mr. Terry. Will you still need the _____?
T: Yes, but I'll have to make it another time. I'll tell you then.
A: Ok. I hope the fog will lift, Mr. Terry.

Activity 2: Writing Task
Write a confirmation letter according to Conversation 1.

Activity 3: Translation
1. I am calling to reserve a presidential suite.
2. Please reserve all six rooms under the name Ray.
3. Should we fax or e-mail the confirmation?
4. We apologize for any inconvenience.
5. We can offer you the special rate of 1000 *yuan* per night.

Unit 2　Guest Check-in

Lead-in Activity

Look at the pictures and discuss the questions.

- Where does the check-in take place?
- When can the guests check in?
- Have you ever checked in/out in a hotel?

◆ Unit 2 Guest Check-in

Job Description

▶▶ Receptionist

- Complete check-in and check-out procedures;
- Allocate rooms and hand out keys;
- Prepare bills and take payments;
- Guide guests to their rooms;
- Deal with complaints or problems.

Conversation

Conversation 1

Checking in Guests with a Reservation

(Scene: Amanda is now checking in a guest with a reservation at the reception desk.)
(A= Amanda, Receptionist; J= John, Guest)

A: Good morning. How may I help you?
J: Good morning. I am here for the international conference.
A: Very good, sir. Do you have a reservation?
J: Yes, in the name of John Smith.
A: Let me check. Yes, a single room. Please fill out the registration form, sir.
J: All right. What floor is it on?
A: The 25th. That's our VIP floor, Room 2509. May I have a look at your passport, please?
J: Certainly. Where is the business center?
A: It's over there on the first floor, right through those doors.
J: Thank you. Do you have a list of the services you offer?

New Words
fill out 填写
registration n. 登记
passport n. 护照

酒店情境英语（上）

A: Yes, here is the brochure with all the details. Would you mind signing the hotel register?
J: Not at all. Is that everything?
A: Yes. Here is your room card.
J: Thank you.
A: I'll call the bellboy to help you with your baggage.

brochure *n.* 小册子
baggage *n.* 行李

Conversation 2

Checking in Walk-in Guests

(Scene: Amanda is now checking in a walk-in guest at the reception desk.)
(A= Amanda, Receptionist; M= Mr. Morris, Guest)

A: Good afternoon, sir. What can I do for you?
M: Good afternoon. I want a room for tonight.
A: Have you made a reservation, sir?
M: I am afraid not.
A: So what kind of room would you like, sir?
M: I need a family room. We are two adults and two children.
A: Ok, we've got a family room left. It's 1200 *yuan* for one night.
M: That's good. We'll take it.
A: You'll need to fill out this form and sign our register.
M: Certainly. By the way, when is breakfast served?
A: It's between 8:00 a.m. and 10:00 a.m. on the 3rd floor.
M: Ok, great.
A: Here is your room card, sir. Room 601. The elevator is straight ahead.
M: Thank you.
A: You're welcome. Hope your family enjoy your stay here.

New Words

walk-in *adj.* 未经预约而来的
elevator *n.* 电梯
straight *adv.* 笔直地

Conversation 3

Extending the Stay

(Scene: Mr. Smith wants to extend his stay in the hotel and Amanda is now helping him.)
(A= Amanda, Receptionist; S= Mr. Smith, Guest)

A: Good afternoon, sir. How may I help you?
S: Good afternoon. I want to extend my stay here for one more night.
A: May I have your name and room number, please?
S: Yes, John Smith in Room 2509.
A: Please wait a moment, Mr. Smith. Let me check the computer record.
S: Ok.
A: I am sorry, Mr. Smith. Your room is not available tonight.
S: Will there be other rooms available?
A: One moment, please. Oh, yes. You got lucky, Mr. Smith. One of our guests is checking out today, and there is no booking so far.
S: That's great. What kind of room is it?
A: It's exactly like yours, with the same rate and everything. Room 1803.
S: Great.
A: Your room card please, Mr. Smith?
S: Here you are. Would you please ask the bellboy to carry my baggage?
A: Of course. Here is your new room card.
S: Thank you so much!
A: You're always welcome.

New Words

extend v. 延长,延伸
record n. 记录
available adj. 可利用的;有空的
check out 退房结账

Useful Words and Expressions

gender 性别   Are you going to check in? 您是要办理入住登记吗?

酒店情境英语（上）

initial 首字母

In whose name was the reservation made?
请问是以哪位的名义做的预订？

facility 设施

How many people are there in the group?
请问您一共几位？

occupation 职业

Please let me know if you require anything else.
如果您还有其他需要，请告知我。

upgrade 升级

Thank you for staying with us. 谢谢您的惠顾。

arrival list 到客名单

I've made a reservation and I'd like to check in.
我已经做了预订，我想现在办理入住。

group visa 团体签证

Should I sign my name here? 我是在这儿签名吗？

visa number 签证号

Do you have any vacancies? 你们这里还有空房吗？

validity date 有效期

Can I get online in my room? 我的房间可以上网吗？

traveler's check 旅行支票

Can I go up to the room now? 我现在可以入住了吗？

Practical Form

Registration Form 入住登记表

Please complete in capital letters 请您用大写字母填写

Personal Information: 个人信息：

First name: 名字：   Last Name: 姓氏：

No. of Adults: 成人数：   No. of Children: 小孩数：

Address: 地址：

Zip Code: 邮编：   Country: 国籍：

Parking: 停车   Yes 是   No 否   License Plate No.: 车牌号：

Identification (Driver's License/Passport Number): 身份证/驾照/护照号码）：

Signature: 签名：

Payment: 支付方式：

☐ Cash 现金

☐ Credit Card 信用卡

☐ Traveler's Check 旅行支票

◆ Unit 2 Guest Check-in

To be completed by reception: 以下内容由接待员填写：	
Name: 姓名：	Arrival Date: 抵店日期：
Departure Date: 离店日期：	Room No.: 房间号
Rate: 房费：	No. of Guests: 客人数：
☐ Continental Breakfast 欧陆式早餐 ☐ Full Breakfast 全套早餐 ☐ Half Board 半食宿 ☐ Full Board 全食宿	

Room Adjustment Form 客房调整表

Day 星期 _____   Date 日期 _____

Room No. 房间号	Room Type 房型	Guest Name 姓名	Period to be Adjusted 需作调整的日期		Remarks 备注
			From 自	To 至	

Ref: 备注：
N/R	未经预订,直接抵店	=Non-Reservation (Walk-in)
Ext.	延期离店	=Extension (Overstay)
Cnl.	取消预订	=Cancellation
Ux-dep	提前离店	=Unexpected Departure (Understay)
Ns	已订房,但未抵店	=No show

酒店情境英语（上）

Abbreviations and Technical Terms

ABF: American Breakfast 西式早餐 A Buffet Breakfast 自助早餐	**BBQ:** Buffet Barbecue 自助烧烤
BF: Buffet 自助餐 Breakfast 早餐	**CBF:** Chinese Breakfast 中式自助早餐
AP: American Plan (breakfast, lunch and dinner) 美式计价	**MAP:** Modified American Plan (breakfast and either lunch or dinner) 修正美式计价
EP: European Plan (no meals) 欧式计价	**DP:** Deposit 押金
FIT: Fully Independent Traveler 散客	**OO:** Out of Order 维修房
EA: Early Arrival 早到	**D.N.A.:** Do Not Arrive (No Show) 客人未到
CL: Clean 干净客房	**OC:** Occupied Room 占用房
CMOP: Complimentary 免费房	**C/I:** Check In 入住办理
No Show: 空订	**C/O:** Check Out 离店办理

Knowledge

Basic Procedure for Check In

- Greeting the guests
- Confirming reservations
- Checking passports/ ID cards
- Registering the guests
- Confirming payment
- Assigning room cards
- Calling the bellboy
- Extending best wishes

Front-Desk Check In

Guests who check in at a hotel all want to be quickly assigned to a room. Typically speaking, guests always present themselves at the front desk to begin the check-in procedure. In some star hotels, a special check-in area may be established for the VIP guests. No matter where the check-in area is, it is always important that staff working in the front desk confirm the room status before assigning them to the guests. Clearly, they should never assign a room that has not been cleaned or that is still occupied to a new arrival.

It is obvious that staff who are responsible for cleaning and inspecting rooms should be in close contact with the front desk so that the room status can be updated continuously throughout the day.

Exercises

Speaking Practice

Activity 1: Discussion

What role does a receptionist play in a hotel? Write down your answers and then discuss with your partners.

Activity 2: Role-play

Role-play 1

Guest: You are a business traveler. You have just checked in but are not satisfied with your room because it is too dark. You would like to change your room.

Clerk: You are the receptionist. You can offer to upgrade the guest's room.

Role-play 2

Guest: You are a walk-in guest. You want a single room for 3 nights, from Oct. 13th to 16th.

Clerk: You are the receptionist. Tell the guest your hotel is fully booked, and recommend a nearby hotel to the guest.

Listening and Writing

Activity 1: Blank Filling—Changing the Room

Listen and fill in the blanks.

R: Good morning, sir. How may I help you?

G: Yes, I have to change my room.

R: May I know the reason, sir?

G: The room was _____ for me. I couldn't sleep all night. I need a quieter room.

R: I am sorry to hear that, sir. May I know your name and room number?

G: I'm Kevin in Room 906.

R: Ok. What about 508, sir? It's very quiet, and has a _____ of the garden.

G: Ok. That will do.

R: Please fill out the _____, sir.

G: Here it is.

R: Would you please return your room card? And here is the room card for Room 508.

G: Thank you.

R: I'll _____ with you. He can help you with your baggage.

G: Fine. That's very kind of you.

R: Not at all. Sorry for the inconvenience. Wish you a _____ tonight!

Activity 2: Writing Task

Fill in the Registration Form according to conversation 1.

Activity 3: Translation

1. Will that be acceptable to you?

2. I am sorry your flight was delayed.

3. Here are the vouchers for your breakfast.

4. Is there any discount if I stay here several days?

5. We will put you in a deluxe suite at no extra charge.

Unit 3 Concierge Service

Lead-in Activity

Look at the pictures and discuss the questions.

- Who helps you with your baggage when you arrive at the hotel?
- What do you know about the position *concierge*?
- What does "one place, for everything" in the above picture mean?

酒店情境英语（上）

Job Description

▶▶ **Concierge**

- Help guests with baggage;
- Advise on hotel facilities;
- Give directions;
- Suggest restaurants;
- Arrange taxis and book tickets;
- Give advice on city tours;
- Run errands, such as picking up dry cleaning.

Conversation

Conversation 1

Receiving and Escorting a Guest

(Scene: Tammy has just arrived at the hotel. The bellboy Raymond receives her. After she checks in, Raymond escorts her to her room.)

(R=Raymond, Bellboy; T= Tammy, Guest)

R: Good evening, madam. Welcome to our hotel. May I help you with your baggage?

T: Yes, please.

R: This way's to the reception counter, please.

Five minutes later, after Tammy checks in...

R: Would you come this way to the lift, please? After you, madam.

T: Thank you.

R: Did you have a good trip?

T: Yes, but I am too tired. I want a good sleep.

New Words

escort *v.* 护送
counter *n.* 柜台
lift *n.* 电梯

Unit 3 Concierge Service

R: I'm sure you'll get it in our hotel. Our rooms are very quiet.
T: That's great.
R: This is the fifth floor, after you.
T: Thank you.
R: This is your room, madam. May I have your room card, please?
T: Of course, here you are.
R: May I put your suitcases here?
T: Sure. You've got wonderful rooms.
R: Thank you, madam. If you need anything, just call us. Wish you a sound sleep.
T: Thank you for all your help.

suitcase *n.* 手提箱
sound *adj.* 酣睡的

Conversation 2

Ticket Booking Service

(Scene: Leo wants to go to the theatre to enjoy the musicals, and William is helping him book the tickets.)
(W=William, Concierge; L= Leo, Guest)

W: Good afternoon, sir. How can I help you?
L: My wife and I want to go to a musical, but we don't know where we can buy tickets.
W: Ok, sir. Do you know what play you want to see?
L: Yes. We are eager to see "Cats."
W: That's a great show, but it's been sold out for several days.
L: Oh, that is so disappointing!
W: Don't worry, sir. Maybe I can pull some strings.
L: Really?
W: Yes, sir. Is a matinee performance ok?
L: Yes, it is ok.
W: Are balcony seats acceptable?
L: It's fine if you can get the tickets.
W: Ok, I'll make some phone calls and get back to you later.
L: That would be a great help! Thank you so much!
W: You are always welcome, sir.

New Words
musical *n.* 音乐剧
sell out 卖完
matinee *n.* 日场演出
balcony *n.* 阳台；包厢

酒店情境英语（上）

Conversation 3

Advising about Tours

(Scene: Jimmy is done with all his business meetings and wants to tour the city. Bill is now giving him advice.)

(J = Jimmy, Guest; B = Bill, Concierge)

J: Hi, Bill. I am finally finished with all my business meetings! I want to see the city.

B: Good idea. What kind of things do you want to see?

J: What do you recommend?

B: Are you interested in modern attractions or historical sites?

J: Historical sites are more for me.

B: Ok, how about the Beijing One-Day Tour?

J: That's great. What's on it?

B: It covers the Great Wall, the Ming Tombs, the Forbidden City and the Tian'an Men Square.

J: How much is it?

B: Well, it costs about 2000 *yuan*.

J: That sounds a little expensive.

B: Yes, but the price includes a private car with a driver and an experienced tour guide.

J: Ok, I'll take it.

New Words

tour *v.* 旅游，观光
recommend *v.* 推荐
attractions *n.* 旅游胜地
historical *adj.* 与历史有关的
private *adj.* 私人的

Useful Words and Expressions

souvenir 纪念品   Shall I arrange a taxi for you, madam?
需要我替您叫一辆出租车吗，女士？

boutique 精品店   The taxi is expected to be here in 15 minutes.
出租车大概在15分钟后到这儿。

itinerary 旅行计划   Here's the timetable of all the tours.
这是所有观光旅行的时间表。

Unit 3 Concierge Service

stopover 中途停留

gourmet food 美食

tennis match 网球赛

museum shop 博物馆纪念品店

novelty gift 新颖的礼品

sight seeing bus 观光巴士

shopping center 购物中心

Is there something I can help you with?
有什么可以帮您的吗?

I can direct you to some good shops.
我可以告诉您一些好的商店。

I have just the place for you.
我有您想要去的地方。

The restaurant is the best in town.
那家餐厅是全城最好的。

I'd like to see a traditional opera.
我想看一场传统歌剧。

I'll need some information about the concerts.
我想了解一些关于音乐会的信息。

I'd like to try some great local cuisine.
我想尝一下当地的美食。

Practical Form

Shuttle Bus Booking Daily Record 班车日报表

Room No. 房号	
Guest Name 宾客姓名	
Route(P/U&D/O) 用车内容	
Flight No. 航班号	
Time 时间	
Terminal 航站楼	
PAX&PCS 人数及件数	
Bellman 行李员	
Driver 司机	
Guest Signature 宾客签字	
Remarks 备注	

酒店情境英语（上）

Baggage Registration Form 行李入住登记表

Date: 日期：_____   Day: 星期：_____

Name of the Group: 团队名称：
_____

Baggage Arr: 行李到达时间： _____	Car No.: 行李车号： _____	List: 客房分配单号： _____
Bagg. Up: 行李送往客房时间： _____	Porter: 卸车行李员： _____	Group No.: 团队编号： _____
No. of Bagg.: 行李件数 _____	No. of Pax: 团队人数： _____	Travel Agency: 旅行社： _____
Handled by: 行李员： _____	Supervised by: 监督员： _____	Captain: 大厅领班： _____

Remarks: 备注：
_____

Abbreviations and Technical Terms

CON: Concierge 礼宾部

EO: Executive Office 行政办公室

EF: Executive Floor 行政楼层

EOD: Executive On Duty 当值行政人员

GRO: Guest Relation Office 客户关系部

GSA: Guest Service Assistant 宾客服务助理

N/L: No Luggage 无行李

TIPS: To Insure Prompt Service 小费，赏金

IHA: International Hotel Association 国际酒店协会

UICH: Union Internationale des Concierges d'Hôtels 国际酒店金钥匙组织

Knowledge

Rules for Great Customer Service

◆ Look neat and clean.
◆ Be customer friendly.
◆ Be aware of your tone & your body language.
◆ Listen attentively.
◆ Maintain eye contact.
◆ Respectful of guests' privacy.
◆ Always provide what you promise.
◆ Never argue with the guests.
◆ Deal with guests' complaints.
◆ Always take the extra step.

Les Clefs d'or (The Golden Keys)

Les Clefs d'or (The Golden Keys), formed in France in October 1929, is a professional association for the hotel concierge staff. It now has more than 3000 members in over 50 countries.

Les Clefs d'or concierges are prudent, patient and kind toward guests and staff alike. They are self-confident, tenacious, persistent, adaptable, ingenious, disciplined, and flexible.

The concierges are motivated by a genuine desire to serve. One can easily recognize them by the keys they display on the lapels of their uniforms. These crossed golden keys are more than just a symbol of the organization—they are the symbol of guaranteed quality service.

酒店情境英语（上）

Exercises

Speaking Practice

Activity 1: Discussion

Are you interested in becoming a concierge? Do you think the job is quite challenging? Write down your answers and then discuss with your partners.

Activity 2: Role-play

Role-play 1

Guest: You are Sophie. You've bought some souvenirs yesterday, and tomorrow you want to shop for yourself.

Clerk: You are the concierge. You give Sophie some recommendations for shopping in town.

Role-play 2

Guest: You are Jack. You would like to choose a gourmet restaurant and you want the restaurant to be romantic.

Clerk: You are the concierge. You recommend the romantic restaurant to Jack, and make the reservation for him.

Listening and Writing

Activity 1: Blank Filling—Advising on Car Rental

Listen and fill in the blanks.

- **R:** Good afternoon, sir. How may I help you?
- **K:** Yes, I'd like to rent a car for next week.
- **R:** No problem. We work with _____.
- **K:** Good. What kinds of cars do you have?
- **R:** We have Honda, Citroen, Toyota, Ford, BMW and Benz.
- **K:** Ok, I think I'll take the New Focus.
- **R:** No problem. But may I have a look at your _____, please?
- **K:** Yes, here it is.

R: Thank you, sir. The price is _____ per day. How long will you need the car?
K: For three days.
R: Ok, we'll need 200 *yuan* as a _____.
K: May I see the car first before I rent it?
R: Yes, of course. I'll _____ it for you.
K: Thank you so much.

Activity 2: Writing Task

Design a modern attraction tourist line in your city for the guests.

Activity 3: Translation

1. Please arrange a taxi for me at 8 tomorrow morning.
2. Do you know a good place to buy some souvenirs?
3. I suggest you a walking tour around the city.
4. That memorial is definitely worth visiting.
5. Please show your baggage claim card when you pick up your baggage.

Unit 4 Telephone Service

Lead-in Activity

Look at the pictures and discuss the questions.

- Do you like talking on the phone?
- Do you know how to leave a phone message?
- What does an operator do everyday?

Unit 4 Telephone Service

Job Description

▶▶ Telephone Operator

- Answer all incoming calls;
- Connect calls to requested extensions;
- Take and pass on messages;
- Provide wake-up call service to the guests;
- Maintain and update telephone directories;
- Answer all guests' questions.

Conversation

Conversation 1

Making a Wake-up Call

(Scene: John needs a wake-up call for tomorrow morning. Monica is helping him.)
(M= Monica, Operator; J=John, Guest)

M: Good evening. This is the operator. How may I help you?
J: Yes. Can you wake me up tomorrow morning?
M: Very well, sir. May I have your room number, please?
J: Room 1502.
M: Ok. What time do you want me to call you?
J: At 6:00 sharp.
M: No problem, sir. What kind of call would you like, by phone or by knocking at the door?
J: I prefer by phone.
M: Ok, sir. Anything else?
J: Yes, are there any messages for me?

New Words
wake-up *adj.* 叫醒的
sharp *adv.* 准时地
knock at 敲（门、窗等）
prefer *v.* 较喜欢

酒店情境英语（上）

M: Let me see, Room 1502. There is so far no message for you, sir.
J: Ok, thanks. Good night.
M: Good night, sir. Have a good sleep!

Conversation 2

Taking a Message

(Scene: Frank wants to talk to Mr. Barry, but no one answers the phone in the room. Monica is answering the phone and taking a message.)
(M= Monica, operator; F= Frank, Guest)

M: Good afternoon, ABC Hotel operator. What can I do for you?
F: Good afternoon. I'd like to speak with Mr. Barry, a guest of yours.
M: Certainly, sir. Do you know his room number?
F: Yes, Room 708. I called his room, but no one answered. May I leave a message for him?
M: Of course, sir. Go ahead, please.
F: I want to invite Mr. Barry to a lunch tomorrow noon. I'll meet him in your hotel lobby at 11.
M: Ok, may I have your name, sir?
F: Yes, it's Frank.
M: May I repeat? Frank invited Mr. Barry in Room 708 for lunch tomorrow and will meet him in our hotel lobby at 11.
F: Yes, exactly!
M: I'll make sure Mr. Barry gets the message.
F: Thank you.
M: You are welcome, sir. Thank you for calling us. Goodbye.

New Words
invite *v.* 邀请
lobby *n.* 酒店大堂

Conversation 3

Making a Long-distance Call

(Scene: Kenneth wants to make a long-distance call. Monica is now helping him with it.)
(M= Monica, Operator; K= Kenneth, Guest)

K: Good morning. This is Kenneth from Room 907.
M: Good morning, sir. How may I help you?
K: Yes, I'd like to make a domestic long-distance call.
M: Certainly, sir. Where to?
K: Nanjing, in Jiangsu Province.
M: Ok. You dial "9," then the "area code," then the number.
K: What's the area code for Nanjing?
M: It's "025," sir.
K: What will the charge be?
M: It's 40 cents per minute.
K: Can I charge it to my room?
M: Certainly, sir.
K: I got it. Thank you very much for your help.
M: Not at all. Have a nice day, sir.

New Words

long-distance *adj.* 长途的
domestic *adj.* 国内的
dial *v.* 拨号
area code 电话区号

Useful Words and Expressions

hold 握住

press 按

button 按钮

speakerphone 免提

cordless phone 无绳电话机

Can I take a message?
需要我传话吗?

Would you like to leave a message?
您要留个口信吗?

I'll put you through in a minute.
我马上为您接通电话。

Can you hold on a moment?
请您稍等一下。

Could you speak a little louder, please?
您能稍微大点儿声吗?

酒店情境英语（上）

hang up 挂断电话

voice mail 语音信息

call waiting 等待电话

phone directory 电话簿

country code 国家代码

The connection was bad.
信号不好。

I have an urgent message for you.
您有个很重要的口信。

There is no reply from Room 1302.
1302房间没有人接听电话。

I can barely hear you.
我几乎听不到您在说什么。

I was cut off in the middle of the call.
我的电话在通话中被切断了。

Practical Form

Message 留言单

Mr/Mrs/Miss
先生/太太/小姐 _____

Time
时间 _____

Message Left by
留言者 _____

Tel.
电话号码 _____

□ Telephoned 来电
□ Returned Your Call 已复电您
□ Will Call Again 将再打来
□ Please Return Call at Tel. _____ 请您回电话给 _____
□ Stopped by to See You 曾到访
□ Urgent 有急事找您

Message 留言：
_____
_____
_____
_____

Message Taken by 记录 _____

Wake Up Call List 叫醒服务

Room No. 房间号码					
Guest Name 宾客姓名					
Confirmation No. 确认号码					
W/U Time 叫醒时间					
2nd W/U Time 第二次叫醒时间					
Taken by 接受人					
Time Received 接受时间					
Informed By 通知人					
Remarks 备注					

Abbreviations and Technical Terms

IDD: International Direct Dialing 国际直拨　　**DDD:** Domestic Direct Dialing 国内直拨

LDD: Local Direct Dial 市话直拨　　**OPR:** Operator 接线员

Long Distance Calls: 长途电话　　**Local Calls:** 市内电话

Collect Calls: 对方付费电话　　**Pay Calls:** 发话人付费电话

Person-to-person Calls: 叫人电话　　**Morning Call:** 叫早服务

酒店情境英语（上）

Knowledge

Telephone Manners

◆ Answer all calls before the third ring.
◆ Be warm and enthusiastic.
◆ Welcome callers courteously and identify yourself and your hotel.
◆ Speak slowly and clearly, while keep your voice volume moderate.
◆ Don't use slangs or buzzwords.
◆ Take messages completely and accurately.

Tech Trends: In-Room Telephones

Nowadays, VoIP (Voice over Internet Protocol 网络语音电话) technology is a move that much in-room telephone development has focused on. Yet there are still other ways to continue satisfying the guests, such as upgrading the telephone hardware.

Bittel Americas, the number one hotel telephone & connectivity panel manufacturer, has brought us one such improvement. They integrate the phone, alarm and dock with a USB port in the hotel.

This integrated device was recently developed out of the concern that it was hard to put an iPhone or iPad on the nightstand and have them connected conveniently to a USB charge port. They recognized this as a universal issue for all hotels and decided to do something about it. The company also is looking at further integrations of telephones with other devices in hotels.

Unit 4 Telephone Service

Exercises

Speaking Practice

Activity 1: Discussion

What kinds of qualifications does one need to be an operator? Write down your answers and then discuss with your partners.

Activity 2: Role-play

Role-play 1

Guest: You are a new guest. You want to make an international long-distance call. But you don't know how to make it.

Clerk: You are the operator. You politely tell the guest in details how to make the call.

Role-play 2

Guest: You are Mr. White. You want to order a wake-up call at 7:00 tomorrow morning. You call the operator to ask for help.

Clerk: You are the operator. You help Mr. White to set up the wake-up call with the computer wake-up service in his room.

Listening and Writing

Activity 1: Blank Filling—Place the Call for the Guest

Listen and fill in the blanks.

O: Good afternoon. This is the operator. How may I help you?

G: Yes. I'm calling a number in Shanghai, but I can't understand what they're saying.

O: That's ok, sir. Let me help you with it. What number are you calling please?

G: _____.

O: Is this a _____?

G: No, it's a company number.

O: May I have the name of the company, please?

G: Yes. It's _____.

酒店情境英语（上）

O: Who would you like to speak to, please?
G: It's Mr. Yang from the HR Department.
O: Do you know his _____?
G: Yes, it's 6256.
O: May I have your name and room number, please?
G: Yes, George in Room 1406.
O: Ok, please _____ now and I'll call you back later.

Activity 2: Writing Task

Leave a message to Mr. Morris that says Henry called to invite him to a party at the Riverside Restaurant at 6:30 tomorrow evening.

Activity 3: Translation

1. I will check the number again.
2. I would like to place a call to Sidney.
3. How do I get an outside line, please?
4. Why don't we hang up and try again?
5. The telephone receiver in his room is not placed in position.

Unit 5 Business Center

Lead-in Activity

Look at the pictures and discuss the questions.

- What is the business center in charge of?
- What equipment does the business center have?
- Have you ever asked for any services from the business center?

Job Description

▶▶ Business Center

- Offer Internet, computer access, printing and photocopying services;
- Provide translation and interpretation services;
- Supply secretarial service;
- Offer equipment rental service for special events;
- Provide ticket-booking and convention service, etc.

Conversation

Conversation 1

Ordering Printing and Photocopy Services

(Scene: Ann has some documents to photocopy. Betsy is helping her as Ann demands.)
(B= Betsy, Receptionist; A=Ann, Guest)

B: Good morning, madam. What can I do for you?
A: I have some documents to photocopy.
B: Ok. How many copies would you like?
A: I need 10 copies of this A5 brochure.
B: Ok. Would you like me to adjust the brightness and intensity?
A: Yes, please. I also need 50 copies of this document.
B: How many pages is it?
A: 10 pages, and we have a lot of pictures in this document.
B: In that case, I suggest the halftone dot printing. It's best for pictures, you know.
A: Good. How much do I owe you?

New Words

photocopy v. 复印
brochure n. 宣传册
adjust v. 调整
intensity n. 调度, 强度
halftone n. 半色调, 中间调

Unit 5 Business Center

B: 30 *yuan* per brochure, and 12 *yuan* per page of this document, that's 900 *yuan*.
A: Do I need to sign the bill?
B: Yes, please.

Conversation 2

Ordering Interpretation Services

(Scene: John needs interpretation service. Betsy is offering her help.)
(B=Betsy, Receptionist; J= John Gates, Guest)

B: Good afternoon, Mr. Gates. Is there anything I can do for you?
J: I need an interpreter for our convention.
B: Ok. Let's fill out the form together.
J: Well, we need an interpreter for 2 days.
B: Ok. Which two languages?
J: Chinese and English, please.
B: And what type of convention is it?
J: Sales and marketing on medical equipment.
B: Well, when do you need the service?
J: 3 days later. It's 27th March.
B: Ok. The daily rate is 2000 *yuan*. So that makes it 4000 in total.
J: That sounds reasonable. Shall I pay cash now?
B: Yes, please. Could you sign here, Mr. Gates?
J: Certainly. Thank you very much.
B: It's my pleasure.

New Words
interpreter *n.* 口译者
medical *adj.* 医学的
daily rate 日工资费
reasonable *adj.* 合理的,公道的

Conversation 3

Booking Flight Tickets

(Scene: Riana is helping Tool to book flight tickets for London.)
(R= Riana, Receptionist; T= Tool, Guest)

R: Business Center. How may I help you?

酒店情境英语（上）

T: I'd like to fly to London the day after tomorrow. Could you please book two tickets for me?

R: Certainly, sir. That's 20th October, isn't it?

T: That's right. How many flights to London every day?

R: Five flights. Four in the morning at 3, 7, 9 and 11 o'clock and one at 3 in the afternoon.

T: I'll take the 9 o'clock flight, two economy tickets.

R: Oh, sorry. Economy class tickets for that flight are fully booked. How about the flight at 11?

T: Fine. Is it refundable?

R: Yes, it is. But once the ticket is issued, there will be a 600 *yuan* cancellation charge.

T: Ok. I'll take it.

R: Would you please fill in this form, sir?

T: Sure.

R: Ok. How would you like to pay?

T: By credit card, please.

New Words
economy class 经济舱
refundable *adj.* 可退还的，可偿还的

Useful Words and Expressions

collate 校对，核对

brightness 亮度

sample 样本，样品

staple 用订书钉钉住

scanner 扫描仪

postal 邮政的，邮局的

I'll send this fax at once.
我马上为您发传真。

Here is...
这是……

How many copies do you want, please?
您需要复印多少份呢？

Would you like me to staple them, please?
您需要我帮您装订吗？

Would you please sign your name here?
您可以在这里签名吗？

Could I see your key card, please?
我能看一下您的出入证吗？

Unit 5 Business Center

operational 可操作的

projector 投影仪

video player 视频播放器

digital cameral 数码相机

100 *yuan* per day, service included.
每天100元,包括服务费。

Would you like limited or unlimited access to the Internet?
请问您是需要有限还是无限上网呢?

What time will you want to use...
您什么时候需要用……

I'd like to make sure my plane reservation is in order.
我想确定我预订的机票是否已经办妥了。

Practical Form

Printing & Photocopying Services 打印、复印服务

Dear Guest, 亲爱的顾客:	
Please fill out the form to order printing or photocopying services. 如您需要打印或复印服务,请您填写此表格。	
Name 姓名	Room No. 房间号码
Telephone 电话号码	Date 日期
Deliver to room 是否送到房间 Yes 是	No 否
PRINTING AND PHOTOCOPYING SERVICES 打印和复印服务	
Number of pages 页数	Number of copies 复印份数
Numbers of pages to copy 复印的页码	
Size 尺寸 letter legal executive A4 A5 B5	
Scale to paper size 调整纸张大小 Yes 是	No 否
Printing 印刷 regular 常规打印 duplex 双面打印	
Half toning 半色调 picture 图画 graphic 图表	
Media 打印材料 plain 普通 glossy 光滑 transparency 透明	
Quality 品质 draft 拟稿 normal 标准 high quality 高品质	
Custom requests 定制 color intensity 颜色亮度 collating 校对 binding 装订	
Handled By 经手人	Guest Signature 顾客签字

酒店情境英语（上）

Translation Service 翻译服务

Dear Guest, 亲爱的顾客：
Please complete the form to reserve translation services.
如您需要翻译服务,请填写此表格。

Name 姓名	Room No. 房间号码
Telephone 电话号码	Date 日期
Deliver to room 是否送到房间 Yes 是	No 否

TRANSLATION SERVICES 翻译服务

Languages 语言   original 原语   target language 译入语

Category 类别   literature 文学   legal 法律   business 商务
　　　　　　　technical 科技   medical 医药   engineering 工程

Formatting requests 格式要求
font 字体 宋体   Times New Roman   Calibri   other 其他
size 字号 5   small 4   4   other 其他

Length of document 文件长度 pages 页数   words 字数

Deadline 交稿日期

Notes 备注

Handled By
经手人   　　　　　　　Guest Signature
　　　　　　　　　　　顾客签字

Abbreviations and Technical Terms

PDA: Personal Digital Assistance 个人数字助理　　**VHS:** Video Home System 录像系统

DVD: Digital Video Disk 视频光盘　　**DPI:** Data Processing Installation 数据处理设备

CD-ROM: Compact Disc Read-Only Memory 只读光盘驱动器　　**BC:** Business Center 商务中心

 Unit 5 Business Center

Knowledge

How to Receive Fax for the Guest

◆ Sort out the guest's name and room number which the fax is sent to.
◆ Check the content completeness.
◆ Put them in an envelop, and note down the name and room number.
◆ Register in the "Guest Receiving Faxing List."
◆ Inform the guest when the fax is ready, or ask the porter to send it to the guest room.
◆ Let the guest sign on the "Business Center Service Receipt" and select a payment method.

About Business Center

The Business Center of hotels was used to be the most profitable unit, providing a wide array of services.

Business service is accessible in most high-end hotels, including photocopying, faxing, printing, equipment and conference room service rental, etc. In the past, business travelers frequently needed such services, and their hotel's business center was usually the only place to meet their needs.

The income of a hotel's business center is, to a large extent, linked to the hotel's occupancy rate. Revenues go up in peak seasons and go down in low ones. These days, the trend is for business travelers to carry a laptop with wireless network capability, and more and more have taken telecommunicating devices like mobile phones as their first choice. There is no longer a clear difference between working in the office and working on the go. One outcome is the declining business for hotels' business centers.

酒店情境英语（上）

Exercises

Speaking Practice

Activity 1: Discussion

What do you think a future business center is like?

Activity 2: Role-play

Role-play 1

Guest: You are Mr. White and want to have some documents typed and delivered to your room before 8 p.m.

Clerk: You are a receptionist. Tell Mr. White it is 10 *yuan* per page, show him a sample and ask for his room number.

Role-play 2

Guest: You want to order computer service, but you have no idea about the Internet security in your hotel. You express your concern to the Business Center staff.

Clerk: You greet the client and assure him/her the wireless network is secure and you will completely erase traces of deleted or unwanted files.

Listening and Writing

Activity 1: Blank Filling—Photocopying Services

Listen and fill in the blanks.

- **C:** Good morning, Mr. White. May I help you?
- **W:** I'd like to get some information on the _____ for our conference tomorrow.
- **C:** Certainly, sir. _____.
- **W:** Well, I'd like to book a conference room for 15 people, a _____ and a computer.
- **C:** The conference room is 2500 *yuan* a day, the slide projector is 800 *yuan* a day, and the computer is 1000 *yuan* a day. So it totals 4300 *yuan*.
- **W:** Well, I have a VIP card, and I have been told I could _____ on facilities rental.
- **C:** May I have the card number, please?

W: Sure. It is _____.
C: Ok, Mr. White. It comes to 3870 *yuan*.
W: Good. Could you make sure everything is ready _____?
C: Sure. Is there anything else?
W: No. Thank you.

Activity 2: Writing Task
Write a computer rental service notice.

Activity 3: Translation
1. The rate for the conference room is on a half day basis, 2500 *yuan* per room.
2. Use your room card for Internet connection with unlimited access.
3. Our clerk will send the copies to your room.
4. Would you prefer first class or economy class?
5. We are not allowed to use our guests' memory storage device.

Unit 6   Settling Complaints

Lead-in Activity

Look at the pictures and discuss the questions.

- In what situation may the guest make a complaint?
- Have you ever made any complaints before?
- What should the receptionist do to settle a guest complaint?

Unit 6 Settling Complaints

Job Description

▶▶ Dealing with Complaints

- Apologize to the guest;
- Make a detailed investigation of the complaint;
- Work out a solution to the complaint;
- Follow up with the guest to make sure he/she is satisfied.

Conversation

Conversation 1

Changing a Room

(Scene: Mr. Rosenberg is not satisfied with his room. He is talking with Betsy about a room change.)
(B= Betsy, Receptionist; R=Rosenberg, Guest)

B: Reception. Betsy speaking. How may I help you?
R: This is Mr. Rosenberg. I've just checked in.
B: Is there any problem, sir?
R: Yes. My room is right next to the street.
B: Oh, dear. Did you make a special request on that?
R: Yes, I did, when I made the reservation.
B: I'm awfully sorry, sir. Let me see if I can get you a quieter one.
R: I have some trouble in sleeping and the noise really bothers me.
B: I understand. Please hold on a moment.
R: I'm really unhappy with it!
B: May I suggest Room 307? It's very quiet and has a lovely view of the garden.

New Words
bother v. 打扰, 使……恼怒

酒店情境英语（上）

R: That sounds nice. Do I need to come down to the reception?

B: No. I'll send the bellboy to your room with the new key.

R: Thanks for your help.

B: Please accept our apology. Let me know if you need anything else.

apology *n.* 道歉

Conversation 2

Missing Valuables

(Scene: Mrs. Walter can't find her purse. Betsy is helping her with the matter.)
(B=Betsy, Receptionist; W= Walter, Guest)

B: Good afternoon, Mrs. Walter. What can I do for you?

W: I certainly hope so. My purse is missing!

B: I'm sorry to hear that. When did you notice it was missing?

W: When I was ready to open my room. The room card is in the purse!

B: Could you tell me something about your purse?

W: Yes, it is blue, medium size.

B: Did you have anything of value inside?

W: Yes! My credit card, some cash and my passport!

B: Ok. Where did you take it with you?

W: I went to the fitness center one hour ago.

B: I'll call the fitness center right now.

W: I've already checked with the people there, but they didn't find it.

B: I'm notifying the hotel security now.

W: Thank you.

B: By the way, please call your credit card company to cancel your card as soon as possible.

W: Ah! Thank you for reminding me that.

New Words

medium size 中号尺码
fitness center 康乐部，健身中心
notify *v.* 通知，通告
hotel security 酒店安全部

Conversation 3

Dealing with a Lost Reservation

(Scene: Betsy is dealing with a mistaken reservation made by Fields who is ready to check in.)
(B= Betsy, Receptionist; F= Fields, Guest)

F: Good evening. I'm here to check in. I have a reservation.
B: May I have your reservation number, please?
F: Sure. It's M75633.
B: I have nothing under that number. Let's see if it's under your name.
F: It's under Damien Smith. D as in double, a as in apple...
B: Sorry, sir. Nothing under that name either.
F: I can't believe this. You sent me a confirmation email on 7th March. Check your record.
B: Oh, we did send you an email. You booked a single room.
F: Yes, I did!
B: I'm terribly sorry, sir. Let me check whether there is any single room left.
F: Just make it quick. I'm exhausted from the long flight.
B: I'm sorry, sir. We have no single room left.
F: What?! This is very disappointing!
B: But we can put you into a suite. It's a deluxe room and we won't charge you extra.
F: Ok. That's a lot better.

New Words

mistaken *adj.* 弄错的
exhausted *adj.* 疲惫的，筋疲力尽的
disappointing *adj.* 令人失望的
suite *n.* 套房
deluxe *adj.* 高级的，豪华的

Useful Words and Expressions

criticism 批评

compliment 夸赞，表扬

I'm terribly sorry to hear that.
对此我感到很抱歉。

I'll look into this matter at once.
我会立刻调查此事。

酒店情境英语（上）

fastidious 挑剔的，苛求的	I will speak to our manager about it. 我会向我们经理说明此情况。
annoyed 恼怒的，烦闷的	I will send an engineer straight up to fix it. 我立刻派工程人员来修理它。
feedback 意见反馈	There could have been some mistakes. I do apologize. 我就这些错误向您道歉。
overcharge 多收钱	Perhaps you could tell me what the matter is exactly. 也许您可以告诉我到底发生了什么事情。
unpleasant 讨厌的，令人不愉悦的	To express our regret for the trouble, we offer you… 为了表达我们的歉意，我们为您提供了……
delightful 高兴的，令人愉快的	I assure you that it won't happen again. 我向您保证此事不会再次发生。
boring 枯燥的，无聊的	The light in my room is too dim. 我房间的灯光太暗了。
irritated 激怒的，生气的	I was woken up several times last night by the noise the baggage elevator made. 我昨晚被运送行李的电梯发出的嘈杂声弄醒了好几次。

Practical Form

Complaint Form 投诉记录单

Complaint Form

Name 姓名 _____　　Date 日期 _____
Hotel room number 房间号码 _____
Check-in date 入住日期 _____
Telephone 电话号码 _____
Home Address 家庭住址 _____

Nature of Complaint 投诉类型

☐ Room was not satisfactory　房间问题

Unit 6 Settling Complaints

□ Guest was overcharged 多收费问题
□ Clothes was damaged by laundry 衣物被洗坏
□ Problem with room facilities 客房设备问题
□ Information was misrepresented 信息误传问题
□ Problem with a hotel staff member 酒店员工问题
□ Problem with Check-in/Check-out 入住或退房问题
□ Other _____ 其他 _____

Complaint Details 详细情况

Confirmed 已确认 □

___

Complaint Mail 投诉信

Hotel Manager
ABC Hotel
11 Tianyuan Road
Beijing, 100000

Dear Sir/Madam,
I stayed at your hotel for four nights, from April 5 to April 9. I have to complain about your facilities and services.
I ordered a wake-up call for 6:00 am on April 6. But I didn't received it, which made me late at my teleconference call.
I was irritated that I got the wrong dishes for room service, and I waited another 30 minutes to have the correct ones.
I was disappointed that the swimming pool in the fitness center was under renovation. I was looking forward to swimming.

I have your VIP card which as I know could offer 10% discount of room rate in low season. But I didn't enjoy the discount although April is just in low season. I feel I should be compensated for this.

Sincerely,

Bruce Kelly

Abbreviations and Technical Terms

GM: General Manager 总经理	**DGM:** Deputy General Manager 副总经理
AM: Assistant Manager 大堂副理	**RM:** Resident Manager 驻店经理
MOD: Manager On Duty 值班经理	**SUPV:** Supervisor 主管
GSTS: Guest Satisfaction Tracking System 宾客意见调查系统	**QES:** Quality Evaluation System 质量评估系统
TQM: Total Quality Management 全面质量管理	**SOP:** Standard Operating Procedures 标准处理程序
DMS: Destination Management System 目标管理系统	**PMS:** Property Management System 酒店经营管理系统

Knowledge

Tips for Dealing with Complaints

◆ Respond quickly
◆ Self confidence
◆ Respect the guest
◆ Be positive
◆ Be considerate

Unit 6 Settling Complaints

Procedures for Settling Complaints

Appropriate response to customer complaints is crucial if you want to maintain an excellent service reputation. When complaints are handled effectively with professionalism in a customer-focused mindset, you have a better chance to earn your customers' forgiveness and their repeat stay. This will mean more business. Here are some suggestions that may help you to be more successful.

- ◆ Reply to the customer immediately in an apologetic tone;
- ◆ Find out more about the customer's complaints and thank the customer for his or her feedback;
- ◆ Express your care and your willingness to solve the complaints;
- ◆ Keep in mind that the customer is always right;
- ◆ Ask the customer whether he or she is satisfied with the ways you solve the complaints, if not, try a different approach which may make him or her happy;
- ◆ Express that you will check out the matter to ensure it won't happen again, and you are looking forward to serving them again.

Exercises

Speaking Practice

Activity 1: Discussion

What do you think a hotel should do in order to reduce the guests' complaints? List your suggestions and discuss them with your classmates.

Activity 2: Role-play

Role-play 1

Guest: You call the Front Office to complain that one piece of your baggage hasn't been sent to your room yet.

Clerk: You are the receptionist. Apologize to Mr. Bell, check with the Bell Captain, and ask questions concerning his baggage and send it to his room.

Role-play 2

Guest: The hairdryer in your room isn't working. And no one has come up to fix it even after being informed. You are complaining to the clerk.

Clerk: You are the receptionist. Apologize to Mr. Black and send another hairdryer to his room.

Listening and Writing

Activity 1: Blank Filling—Guest Complaints about the Equipment

Listen and fill in the blanks.

C: Front Office. May I help you?

B: Yes, the _____ in my room is _____ and the water won't go down.

C: I'm terribly sorry to hear that. May I have your name and room number.

B: _____ in Room 401.

C: OK. Please wait a moment, Mr. White. I will send the _____ to fix it right away.

B: Please be quick. I have to leave in five minutes.

C: Ok. Do you mind if _____?

B: No. I hope you get it fixed well before I come back.

C: No problem. Mr. White. We do _____.

B: That's OK.

C: Please don't hesitate to telephone us if you have any other problem.

Activity 2: Writing Task

Write a reply to the Complaint Mail as the manager of ABC Hotel.

Activity 3: Translation

1. I'd like to complain to your manager.
2. We promise to make your room first next time.
3. This sweater was ruined by your laundry room. Your service is unbelievable.
4. If you need anything else, please let us know.
5. The room next door is too noisy and it's a headache.

Unit 7 Guest Check-out

Lead-in Activity

Look at the pictures and discuss the questions.

- Where does a guest go to check out?
- What does a check-out receptionist do everyday?
- Have you ever encountered any problems during checkouts?

酒 店 情 境 英 语 （上）

Job Description

▶▶ Receptionist

- Exchange money for guests;
- Ask the guest to settle the bill;
- Explain the items charged in the bill;
- Update the room status;
- Complete check-out procedures.

Conversation

Conversation 1

Exchanging Foreign Currency

(Scene: Alberto is exchanging dollars for euros.)
(A= Alberto, Guest; K=Kevin, Receptionist)

K: Good morning, sir. How may I help you?
A: I'd like to exchange some currency, please.
K: Certainly, sir. What currency are you selling?
A: I'd like to exchange 300 US dollars into euros.
K: May I see your I.D. card or your passport, please?
A: Here is my passport. What's today's exchange rate?
K: It's 1 US dollar to 0.74 euro at the moment.
A: Ok. I'd also like to exchange 200 US dollars for RMB.
K: No problem, sir. 6.16 RMB to 1 dollar.
A: Any service charge?
K: Yes. We charge 30 *yuan* for each transaction.
A: That sounds reasonable. May I have a receipt, please?

New Words

exchange *v.* 兑换
currency *n.* 货币
exchange rate 汇率
service charge 酬金，劳务费

K: Yes, sir. Here is your money. Would you please sign the receipt?
A: Sure.

Conversation 2

Checking out for the Guest

(Scene: Mr. Walter is checking out at the reception.)
(B=Betsy, Receptionist; W= Walter, Guest)

B: Good afternoon, sir. May I help you?
W: Yes, I'd like to check out now.
B: May I have your name and room number, please?
W: My name's Walter. Room 615. Here is the key.
B: I'm very sorry, Mr. Walter. But we have to add the cost of the bed sheet to your bill.
W: How much is it?
B: It is $100. Here is your bill. It totals $1000.
W: Can I pay with my credit card?
B: Of course, Mr. Walter.
W: May I have the receipt?
B: Certainly. Here is your receipt, sir.
W: Thank you.
B: I hope you enjoyed your stay here, Mr. Walter.

New Words
bed sheet 床单

Conversation 3

Amending a Guest Bill

(Scene: Ms. Moore is checking out, and there is something wrong with the bill.)
(A= Amanda, Receptionist; M= Ms. Moore, Guest)

M: Good afternoon, I'd like to check out now.
A: Good afternoon, madam. May I have your name and room number?
M: Sheilla Moore. Room 309.
A: Very well, Ms. Moore. Let me prepare your bill. Here it is.

酒店情境英语（上）

M: Er... There might be something wrong on the bill.
A: Oh, yes?
M: I checked in on 10th and will leave this afternoon. That's exactly seven nights, but there are eight nights on the bill.
A: Well, I am awfully sorry. I do apologize for my mis-checking.
M: One more thing, I never used the minibar.
A: Oh, let me check with the Housekeeping.
M: I'm in a hurry. I have to catch my flight.

After calling the Housekeeping...

A: I'm sorry, madam. It's our mistake. Is there any other problem?
M: No.
A: Ok. Now let me reprint your bill and invoice.
M: Thank you.

New Words

mis-checking *n.* 入住登记错误
minibar *n.* 迷你吧
reprint *v.* 重印
invoice *n.* 发票

Useful Words and Expressions

account 账户，账单

cashier 收银，出纳员

transfer 转让，转移

signature 签名

refund 退款，偿还

exchange memo 外汇兑换水单

draw up 拟定，起草

guest folio 客人账单

Here is your bill, please check it.
这是您的账单，请您查阅。

Your bill comes to...
您一共消费了……

I'm terribly sorry for overcharging you.
非常抱歉，多收了您的钱。

How would you like to make the payment?
您想怎样付款？

Please sign your name here.
请在这里签上您的名字。

May I leave my bags here until 3 pm?
我可以把行李放在这里吗？我下午3点来取。

Be sure not to leave anything behind, please.
请您检查不要落掉东西。

We hope you had a pleasant stay at our hotel.
希望您在我们酒店住得愉快！

credit limit 信贷限额

one-way change 单向兑换

We look forward to seeing you again.
期待您的下次光临。

Would you like it in small or large bills?
您是想要小额还是大额钞票?

Practical Form

Room Allocation Plan 客房分配表

Room Allocation Plan

Guests checking in on May 9, 2013　　2013年5月9日宾客入住情况

Name 姓名	Room No. 房号	Meal Plan 用餐安排	No. of Adults 成年人数目	No. of Children 儿童数目	Remarks 备注

Handled by 经手人

Guests checking out on May 9, 2013　　2013年5月9日宾客退房情况

Name 姓名	Room No. 房号	Payment 付款方式	Remarks 备注

Handled by 经手人

酒店情境英语（上）

Check-out Bill 离店账单

Name of Guest 客人姓名 _____

Room No. 房号 _____   Room Rate 房价 _____

Arrival Date 入住日期 _____   Departure Date 退房日期 _____

Method of Payment 付款方式
□ Cash 现金   □ Credit Card 信用卡   □ Debit Card 借记卡   □ Other 其他

Date 日期	Charges Details 款项	Remarks 备注	Amount 金额
	Total 合计		

Guest Signature 客人签字
_____

Cashier No. 款台号
_____

Unit 7 Guest Check-out

Abbreviations and Technical Terms

C/O: check out 离店结账	**LCO:** Late check-out 晚退房
C.O.D: Cash Payment on Departure 离店现付	**P.I.A.:** Paid In Advance 已预付
COMP: Complimentary 免费	**R.R:** Average Room Rate 住房平均价
VIP: Very Important Person 贵宾	**EXT:** Extension 延住
LSG: Long Staying Guest 长住客人	**T/T:** Telegraphic Transfer 电汇
ASAP: As Soon As Possible 尽快	**ADJ:** Adjustment 调整
Extra Bed 加床	Repeated Guest 回头客
Connecting 连通房	Permanent Room 长包房
Package 包价	Rack Rate 门市价

Knowledge

Different Payments the Hotel Accept

- Credit card
- Debit card
- Gift certificate
- Money order
- Personal check
- Traveler's check
- Foreign currency

Points for Attention in Check-out

The check-out service is the last step during the guest's stay in a hotel. As has been repeatedly stressed, first and last impressions carry the most weight. Therefore, it's extremely significant for the receptionist to leave a pleasant impression to the guest in order to gain his or her next stay. The warm, courtesy and professional service is a must for the receptionist to gain favorable impressions. Besides, a well-prepared and organized front office is the key to keep the checkout service going smoothly. Generally speaking, close attention should be paid for the following :

◆ Night receptionist should prepare the "Expected Check-out Room List" and items the customers have to pay for the following day to ensure a high speed check-out service.

◆ A pleasant and natural smile is required during the check-out process. Asking for the room number, confirming the name of the customer, settling the bill, explaining the item charge on the bill if necessary and getting back the room key should be operated in high efficiency.

◆If necessary, ask for the customer's feedback.

◆Update the room status and create the new record.

Exercises

Speaking Practice

Activity 1: Discussion

Do you think you're qualified to work at the Check-out Center? What qualities should the receptionist have in order to gain the guest's next stay?

Activity 2: Role-play

Role-play 1

Guest: You are Mr. Bing and want to change 500 US dollars into RMB.

Clerk: You are the receptionist. Give Mr. Bing his bill; tell him the current exchange rate between the U.S. dollar and the RMB is 100: 613 and ask him whether he needs some small change.

Role-play 2

Guest: You come to the cashier's desk to check out. After checking the bill, you find that you are overcharged by 100 *yuan*.

Clerk: You are the cashier. You help Ann to check out. Apologize to her for overcharging and refund the money overpaid.

Listening and Writing

Activity 1: Blank Filling—Guest Check-out

Listen and fill in the blanks.

- B: Good morning, Mr. Zhang. What can I do for you?
- Z: I'd like to _____ now.
- B: Ok. Could I have your room number, please?
- Z: My room number is 1105 and _____.
- B: Please wait a moment while _____.
- Z: Ok.
- B: Here is your bill, Mr. Zhang. It _____. Please check it.
- Z: Ok. But I paid a 4000 *yuan* deposit when I checked in.
- B: May I have the _____, please?
- Z: Of course. Here you are.
- B: Thank you. We'll return 150 *yuan* to you. Please check it and _____.
- Z: Thank you.
- B: It's my pleasure. I hope you enjoyed your stay with us here.

Activity 2: Writing Task

Write a confirmation letter of the check-out date.

Activity 3: Translation

1. We will return the balance to you.
2. Item 5 is the charge for laundry service.
3. We accept American Express, Master Card and Visa.
4. Would you like to check and see if there's any mistake?
5. If you check out after 6 p.m., you'll have to pay full rate.

Unit 8 Chamber Service

Lead-in Activity

Look at the pictures and discuss the questions.

- What can you see from the picture above?
- What service do you think the attendant is offering?
- How to you get this service in a hotel?

Unit 8 Chamber Service

Job Description

▶▶ Room Attendant

- Enter and prepare the room for cleaning;
- Vacuum floors and carpets;
- Make the beds;
- Dust the guestrooms and furniture;
- Change linens;
- Replenish the guestrooms and bath supplies;
- Handle special requests of the guests.

Conversation

Conversation 1

Making up the Room

(Scene: Carol is knocking at Mrs. Smith's door.)
(C= Carol, Room Attendant; S=Mrs. Smith, Guest)

C: Housekeeping. May I come in?
S: Come on in, please.
C: Sorry to disturb you, Mrs. Smith. I'm Carol. Would you like your room cleaned?
S: I'm afraid it's not the time. I'm going to take a bath. Can you come back one hour later?
C: Sure, Mrs. Smith. I'll be back in an hour. You might want to put a "Do Not Disturb" sign on the doorknob.
S: Thank you, Carol. Can you help me put the sign on?
C: It's my pleasure, Mrs. Smith.

New Words
disturb v. 打扰

酒店情境英语（上）

One hour later, there are soft knocks at the door.

C: Housekeeping. May I come in?

S: Come on in, please.

C: Nice to see you again, Mrs. Smith. Can I do your room now?

S: Sure. The bath really refreshed me after an 8-hour flying. But the bathroom is a bit messy now.

C: No worry, Mrs. Smith. I'll clean out the tub and mop the floor at once.

S: The toilet paper and the hair conditioner have been used up.

C: I'll get you a new roll and replenish the bath supplies immediately.

S: That's great!

C: The soiled linens have been removed and fresh towels are ready, Mrs. Smith.

S: Good. Oh, one more thing, if you listen to the bathroom door, it squeaks. The noise is quite annoying.

C: We are very sorry, Mrs. Smith. I'll fix the hinges right away.

> refresh *v.* 消除疲劳，使振作精神
> conditioner *n.* 护发素
> linen *n.* 布草
> squeak *v.* 吱吱叫

Conversation 2

Turn-down Service

(Scene: Mrs. Wilsons is sitting in the room when Carol knocks at the door.)
(C=Carol, Room Attendant; W=Mrs. Wilson, Guest)

C: Housekeeping. May I come in?

W: Yes, please.

C: Good evening, Mrs. Wilson. May I do the turn-down service for you now?

W: Sure, go ahead.

C: Shall I close the drapes for you?

W: Yes, please. That would make the room comfy and cozy. By the way, I had a problem with the pillow last night. I kept sneezing and even couldn't fall asleep.

C: I am awfully sorry to hear that. You must have an allergy to feathers.

W: I guess so.

C: I will bring you a buckwheat pillow immediately. I've

> **New Words**
> turn-down *n.* 做夜床
> drape *n.* 窗帘
> cozy *adj.* 舒适的
> sneeze *v.* 打喷嚏
> allergy *n.* 过敏

folded the corner of the quilt and the slippers are on the little mat by the bed.

W: Thank you. Please switch on the reading lights. I'd like to do some reading in bed.

C: No problem. By the way, besides chocolate, we also offer relaxing spray. You have a choice between lavender and rose mists.

W: Lavender is fine. Thank you for your help.

C: I'm always at your service, Mrs. Wilson. I'll be back in a minute with the new pillow.

lavender *n.* 薰衣草

Conversation 3

Asking for More Articles

(Scene: Mrs. Walter is calling the room attendant for more articles.)

(M= Marcy, Room Attendant; W= Mrs. Walter, Guest)

M: Housekeeping. Marcy speaking. How may I help you?

W: Hello, Marcy. This is Mrs. Walter in Room 809. Can you get me a corkscrew and two flute glasses, please?

M: No problem. I'll send them up to you right away. Do you need anything else, Mrs. Walter?

W: Oh, yes. Can you get us an ice bucket with ice cubes in? That can keep leftover sparkling wine properly chilled.

M: So a wine-opener, two flute glasses and a bucket of ice cubes. Am I correct, Mrs. Walter?

W: That's right. Thank you. Oh, one more thing.

M: Sure.

W: The mini-bar needs refilling, but no more candy bars, please. You know they're bad for kids' teeth.

M: No problem. I'll send someone to refill it right away.

W: Thank you for your help.

M: You are welcome, Mrs. Walter. Have a nice day.

New Words

corkscrew *n.* (拔软木塞用的)螺丝起子
flute glass 长笛形酒杯
bucket *n.* 桶
sparkling *adj.* 起泡的
refill *v.* 再装满,再充满

酒店情境英语（上）

Useful Words and Expressions

chambermaid 女服务员

bedspread 床罩

at your service 愿意为您效劳

vacuum 用真空吸尘器打扫

stationery 文具，办公用品

on shift 值班

prior to 在……之前

remote control 遥控器

overnight staff 夜班员工

hair dryer 吹风机

make the beds
铺床

May I tide up the desk?
我可以擦一下桌子吗？

I'll try and see if I can do something for you.
我会尽力，看一下能否为您做点什么。

You've been very helpful.
您帮了我大忙了。

What time will be better for you, sir?
先生，您什么时间合适？

I have a few special requests.
我有些特殊要求。

I'll get one to you immediately.
我马上给您送一个。

I'll take care of that right away.
我马上着手处理。

I'll have one sent up to you.
我马上给您送一个上去。

You can call the front desk when you want your room done.
您需要打扫房间服务的时候可以致电前台。

Unit 8 Chamber Service

Practical Form

Housekeeping Trolley 客房服务小推车

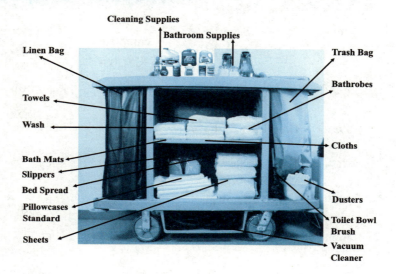

Linen Reuse Card 布草环保使用卡

Serve the Environment

In order to contribute to our environment through the important savings in water, electricity and detergent, we will be changing our guest room bath towels every three nights.

If you wish to join in our program, please put this card on your pillow: **Fresh Towels are NOT Necessary Today.**

Thank you for your participation.

酒店情境英语（上）

Guest Requests Chart 客人要求记录卡

Floor Attendant: David Smith   Date: May 4th, 2013

Time of Request 时间	Room #房号	Request 具体要求	Time completed 完成时间	Chambermaid 经手人	Signature 签字
10:20	824	Cell phone re-charger	10:25	Lucy	
10:40	803	Hair dryer & shaver		Lucy	
11:15	807	Health scale	11:35	Lucy	
12:17	801	More bath towels		Tom	
12:37	806	Restock minibar	12:50	Tom	

Abbreviations and Technical Terms

OOO: Out of Order 待修房

DND: Do Not Disturb 请勿打扰

S/O: Sleep Out 外宿

LSG: Long Staying Guest 长住客人

NB: No Baggage 无行李

LB: Light Baggage 轻行李

C/I: Check In 登记入住

C/O: Check Out 退房

OC: Occupied Clean 干净住客房

OD: Occupied Dirty 脏住客房

VD: Vacant Dirty 脏空客房

VC: Vacant Clean 干净空客房

PMU: Please Make Up 即扫客房

DL: Double Lock 双锁房

GRS: Guest Refuse Service 客人拒绝服务

T/D: Turn-down Service 夜床服务

Unit 8 Chamber Service

Knowledge

Cleaning Path

	Returning later when there is a Do Not Disturb sign on the knob or the door is double-locked from inside.

Entering the Guestroom	**Knocking** on the door twice and announcing "housekeeping" and waiting for guest response.

Beginning Tasks	**Turning** on all the lights and drawing back the draperies;
	Checking the air conditioning and heater;
	Making note of damaged or missing item;
	Collecting any service trays, dishes, bottles or cans;
	Removing dirty ashtrays and glasses and emptying wastebasket.

Making the Bed	**Checking** the mattress pad and the mattress;
	Changing pillowcases and sheets, then mitering;
	Placing the quilt, bedspread and blanket;

| Cleaning the Bathroom | Showering Area → | Vanity & Sink → | Toilet → | Walls & Fixture → | Floor → |

| Dusting | Picture frames, Mirrors, Bedside tables, Telephone, Windowsills, Dresser, Television, Stand, Chairs, Closet, Doors, Knobs, Air conditioning, Heating units, Fans, and Vents. |

| Vacuuming | **Loosening** dirt around with a broom or rag; |
| | **Staring** at the farthest end of the room and vacuuming way back. |

Final Checking	**Giving** the room a careful look from the guest's perspective;
	Making sure that all the furnishings are back in their proper places;
	Turning off the lights;
	Closing the door and locking it;
	Marking a room assignment sheet.

The Role of the Housekeeping Department

Headed by the executive housekeeper, the Housekeeeping Department plays a significant role within a hotel. Housekeeping is a very physically demanding job since the priority of housekeepers is to maintain a spotless appearance in both guest rooms and public areas. What's more, the Housekeeping Department provides the in-house laundry service as well as many other special services.

◆ Unit 8 Chamber Service

   As one of the most integral department of a hotel, the Housekeeping Department is vital to attracting and keeping guests through its role of maintaining top quality decoration, cleanliness and service. Trivial carelessness can upset a guest and thus affect the occupant's impression of the hotel. In a competitive hotel market, small details make a great impact on guests and determine whether they will return.

Exercises

Speaking Practice

Activity 1: Discussion
Do you think you're qualified to work as a room attendant in the housekeeping department? Write down your strengths and weaknesses and then discuss with your partners.

Activity 2: Role-play

Role-play 1
Guest: You are Mr. Baker expecting some friends. Call the front desk for chamber service and ask for a Thermos of hot water and some Chinese tea.
Clerk: You are the front desk clerk. Tell Mr. Baker that you will send a chambermaid up within five minutes to handle his requests.

Role-play 2
Clerk: You are a chambermaid. You're going to do the turn-down service for Mrs. White.
Guest: You are Mrs. White in Room 709. You ask the chambermaid to do every step of the turn-down service except cleaning the bathroom because you haven't taken a bath. What's more, you ask her to bring you an English newspaper.

Listening and Writing

Activity 1: Blank Filling—Dealing with Guest's Request
Listen and fill in the blanks.
C: Housekeeping. Carol speaking. _____?

酒店情境英语（上）

B: Hello, Carol. Would you please do me a favour?
C: Yes, sir. _____.
B: My son is coming for the summer holiday next week.
C: That's great.
B: Yes. I wonder whether I can have an extra bed, a kind of roll-away?
C: Of course, sir. But please contact the _____ first.
B: OK. Any idea how much does an extra bed cost?
C: 120 *yuan* per night.
B: By the way, can you do the turn-down service an hour later?
C: I'm afraid I'll be off then, but I'll _____ right away.
B: That's very kind of you.
C: May I _____ ?
B: Bill Graham in Room 1105. Thanks for your help.
C: _____. Have a pleasant evening.

Activity 2: Writing Task

Write a note to your colleague. Tell her to do the turn-down service for Mr. Graham in Room 1105.

Activity 3: Translation

1. We always serve rooms early on request.
2. What time would be convenient to you?
3. May I move the things on your desk so that I can dust it?
4. Could you please clear the fridge of all the beers and spirits?
5. You can call the front desk when you want your room done.

Unit 9   Laundry Service

Lead-in Activity

Look at the pictures and discuss the questions.

- What is laundry service?
- Have you ever experienced laundry service?
- How do you get the laundry service in a hotel?

酒店情境英语（上）

Job Description

▶▶ Laundry Service

- Collect dirty linens and laundry from the guest rooms;
- Sort the laundry in terms of fabric types and degrees of staining;
- Wash or dry-clean the laundry;
- Iron or repair on guests' request;
- Deliver the laundry.

Conversation

Conversation 1

Explaining How to Get the Service

(Scene: Amy is explaining the laundry service to John.)
(A= Amy, Chambermaid; J=John, Guest)

A: Excuse me. Have you any laundry?

J: No, not now. Thank you.

A: If you have any, please leave it in the laundry bag behind the bathroom door. The valet comes to collect guests' laundry every morning.

J: I see. Could you tell me your laundry service hours?

A: If we receive your laundry before 10 a.m., we'll deliver it to you before 5 p.m. If the laundry is received before 2 p.m., it will be sent back to you the next morning, sir.

J: What about the charge?

A: Here's the price list. Please call us or notify in the list whether you need your clothes ironed, dry-cleaned or mended.

New Words

laundry *n.* 需要洗熨的衣物
valet *n.* 洗熨员
deliver *v.* 递送
iron *v.* 熨平（衣物）

Unit 9 Laundry Service

J: I see. What if there's any laundry damage?
A: In such cases, the hotel should certainly pay for it.
J: That sounds reasonable. I hope there's no damage at all.
A: Don't worry, sir. We have very experienced staff.
J: All right. Thank you for your information.
A: Not at all.

Conversation 2

Providing Express Service

(Scene: Tracy is calling the housekeeping department to get some information about the express service.)
(A= Amy, Housekeeper; T=Tracy, Guest)

T: Hello. Is that housekeeping?
A: Yes, madam. How can I help you?
T: I need to send my silk skirt for dry cleaning. I spilt some red wine on it.
A: No worry, madam. We have excellent laundry service, and soda water usually works really well on red wine stains.
T: How do you separate items for dry cleaning?
A: We of course sort according to the types of items, fiber, color fastness, how soiled the item is, etc.
T: Great! Can I have it back by tomorrow evening? I need it for the classical concert then.
A: Sure. Clothes left by 8:00 a.m. are returned by 6:00 p.m. that evening.
T: But I have to get to the concert hall by 6:00 p.m. Do you have an express service?
A: Yes. But there's a 50% additional charge for that.
T: I guess I don't have a choice. So when will the skirt be returned?
A: By 2:00 p.m., madam. Be sure to write "silk" when you fill out the laundry form.
T: Fine. Please ask them not to fold the skirt. I want it on a hanger.
A: No problem.
T: Excellent. Please send someone up to collect the laundry bag.
A: Right away, madam.

New Words

express service 快洗服务, 加急服务
stain n. 污渍
fastness n. 不褪色
additional adj. 另外的

Conversation 3

Handling Laundry Damages

(Scene: Anna is receiving a phone call from Mr. Smith who is complaining about the laundry damage.)
(A= Anna, Service Center Clerk; F= Frank, Assistant Manager; S= Mr. Smith, Guest)

A: Good afternoon. Anna from the Service Center speaking. How may I help you?

S: This is John Smith. I just received my laundry. But the wool sweater has faded and there are runs in it.

A: We are very sorry, Mr. Smith. I'll send someone up and check it immediately.

5 minutes later

F: Housekeeping. May I come in?

S: Yes, please.

F: Good afternoon, Mr. Smith. I'm the assistant manager. May I have a look at the sweater?

S: Here you are. It's totally ruined.

F: We are terribly sorry, Mr. Smith. The hotel should certainly pay for the damage, but the indemnity is limited to 10 times the charge for cleaning.

S: What's the laundry charge?

F: 30 *yuan*.

S: 30 *yuan*? It means that I can only get 300 *yuan* for compensation? I won't accept it. That's so unfair.

F: Then how about you buy a new sweater here and give us the receipt? We'll refund the cost of the laundry and the new one.

S: Listen! I'm leaving for the airport this afternoon. I won't have time for that.

F: No worry, Mr. Smith. You can buy another one when you go back to America and send us the receipt. We'll send you a bank draft for the amount.

S: That sounds reasonable.

F: We are really sorry for your loss and all the inconvenience, Mr. Smith. Thank you for your understanding.

New Words
indemnity *n.* 赔偿金
compensation *n.* 补偿
receipt *n.* 收据
bank draft 银行汇票

Unit 9 Laundry Service

Useful Words and Expressions

bleach 漂白

iron 熨烫

dry-clean 干洗

stitch 缝补

shrink 缩水

colorfast 不褪色

starch 上浆

dye 染色

tear up 撕裂

per item/load 每件/堆

Refer to your laundry list for further information.
详情请查阅洗衣单。

I'm collecting laundry.
我来收取送洗衣物。

Could you fill out the laundry form?
请您填写洗衣单。

We'll stitch it before washing.
洗衣之前我们会补好。

Will the color run in the wash?
水洗的时候会褪色吗?

When can I have my laundry back?
我送洗的衣物什么时候可以送回?

Express service only takes three hours.
快洗服务只需要三个小时。

Please accept our apology.
请接受我们的道歉。

We'll check if your laundry has come back.
我们会查看您的衣物是否送回。

There's a small problem with your laundry.
您的送洗衣物有点问题。

酒店情境英语（上）

Practical Form

Laundry Form 洗衣表

Name 姓名 _____

Room No. 房号 _____

No. of Pieces 件数 _____

Please Indicate 请标注
☐ Express 加急
☐ Same Date 当天

Shirts Returned 衬衫返回
☐ Folded 折叠
☐ On Hanger 挂架
☐ Starched 上浆

Date 日期

Special Instructions 特别要求
_____
_____

Amount 数量	Gentlemen 男士	Unit Price RMB 单价/元	Amount 数量	Ladies 女士	Unit Price RMB 单价/元
		Washing/水洗			
	Dress shirt 晚礼衬衫	40.00		Dress 连衣裙	50.00
	Shirt 衬衫	35.00		Jacket 外套	50.00
	T-Shirt T恤	30.00		Shirt 衬衫	40.00
	Jacket 外套	50.00		Blouse 女恤	40.00
	Track Suit(2pcs) 运动套装	40.00		T-shirt T恤	35.00
	Trousers/Jeans 裤子/牛仔裤	50.00		Pants/Jeans 裤子/牛仔裤	40.00
	Pajamas(2pcs) 睡衣裤(套)	40.00		Pajamas (2pcs) 睡衣裤(套)	30.00
	Socks 短袜	15.00		Track Suit (2pcs) 运动装(套)	30.00
	Shorts 短裤	20.00		Brassiere 胸罩	30.00
	Undershirt 内衣	15.00		Shorts 短裤	15.00
	Underpants 内裤	15.00		Skirt 半裙	40.00
				Stocking 袜子	15.00

Unit 9 Laundry Service

Dry Cleaning/干洗					
	Suit (3pcs)西装(套)	125.00		Suit (2pcs) 西装（套）	125.00
	Jacket 外套	100.00		Jacket 外套	100.00
	Trousers 西裤	80.00		Dress 连衣裙	60.00
	Overcoat 长大衣	150.00		Skirt(Full Pleat) 百褶裙	60.00
	Silk shirt 丝质衬衣	60.00		Skirt(Regular) 半裙	50.00
	Sweater 毛衣	80.00		Blouse 女恤	40.00
	Tie/Vest/scarf 领带/背心/围巾	30.00		Sweater 毛衣	80.00
				Overcoat 长大衣	160.0
				Scarf 丝巾	30.00
Ironing 净熨					
	Suit (3pcs)西装(套)	80.00		Suit (2pcs) 西装（套）	35.00
				Dress 连衣裙	40.00
	Jacket 外套	60.00		Skirt 半裙	30.00
	Shirt 衬衣	30.00		Jacket 外套	40.00
	Trousers 西裤	30.00		Blouse 女恤	30.00
	Tie 领带	10.00		Slacks 长裤	30.00

This form must be completed and signed by the guest 本单必须由客人填写并签字

Guest's Signature 客人签字_____

Sub Total 小计 _____

Plus 50% Express Charge 加收50%加急费 _____

Plus15% Service Charge 加收15%服务费 _____

Grand Total RMB 总计/元 _____

酒店情境英语（上）

Abbreviations and Technical Terms

Marks on Washing tags 洗衣标识	
dry clean 干洗	hang dry 悬挂晾干
do not dry clean 不可干洗	dry flat 平放晾干
iron 熨烫	do not tumble dry 不可转笼干燥
wash 洗涤	do not wash 不能洗涤
iron on low heat 低温熨烫 (100°c)	hand wash only 只能手洗
iron on medium heat 中温熨烫 150°c	wash with cold water 冷水机洗
iron on high heat 高温熨烫 (200°c)	wash with warm water 温水机洗
do not iron 不可熨烫	wash with hot water 热水机洗
bleach 可漂白	do not bleach 不可漂白

Knowledge

Clothing Materials

- Natural clothing materials include cotton, linen, flax, wool, ramie, silk, denim, leather, down and fur.
- Synthetic fibers include nylon, polyester, elastane, etc.
- Less-common clothing materials include acetate, bamboo, flannel, cupro, etc.

The Hotel Laundry and Valet Service

Besides cleaning guest rooms and public areas, housekeeping departments of many quality hotels provide laundry and valet service. The biggest part of a hotel laundress's job is to deal with hundreds or thousands of towels, sheets, rags, mats, tablecloths and linen napkins that are soiled during a hotel's daily operation. The same is true of the valet service, which cares for the uniforms of the hotel staff.

During their stay, hotel guests may need their clothes washed, dry-cleaned, starched or ironed. Laundry service should be offered in an efficient way to meet guests' different requirements. Standard service time is ten hours. Express service is available for an additional charge. Normally, tipping for laundry service is not necessary, but it will be appreciated if the service is beyond expectation.

Exercises

Speaking Practice

Activity 1: Discussion
Discuss with your partners about the ways to reduce laundry damage in a hotel.

Activity 2: Role-play

Role-play 1

Guest: You are Mr. Baker in Room 1406. You call the service center to find out if you can get laundry service. You want your suit dry-cleaned for there is a grease stain on it and you also want one button sewed.

Clerk: You are the service center clerk and you answer the phone and provide some information about the laundry service to Mr. Baker.

Role-play 2

Guest: You find that your clothes mis-delivered.

Clerk: You are the valet who delivered the laundry. You make an apology to the guest in an appropriate way.

Listening and Writing

Activity 1: Blank Filling—Asking for Laundry Service
Listen and fill in the blanks.

T: Guest room service. How may I help you?

A: Hello. I have a silk dress that needs _____. I spilt some coffee on it and I need to wear it this evening.

T: Mm, we can have it _____ and back to you in one hour. Is that ok?

A: Great. We are not leaving until 7:30.

T: I'll _____ in five minutes to _____ the dress.

A: Oh, by the way. One of the buttons is loose on my husband's suit.

T: I'll tell the valet to sew it for you.

A: Excellent! Do you know how much those items will charge?

T: Well, it's probably easier if you _____. It is in the top drawer of the writing desk.

A: Does it include a price schedule?

T: Yes, madam.

Activity 2: Writing Task
Write a memorandum on the guests' complaints about the laundry service.

Activity 3: Translation
1. I'm missing some buttons from my blouse.
2. I'd like this sweater washed by hand in cold water.
3. I really need an iron and ironing board to press my dress.
4. We will do our best to remove the stain but we cannot guarantee the result.
5. Express service for any urgent laundry or pressing will be done at 50% extra charge.

Unit 10 Maintenance Service

Lead-in Activity

Look at the pictures and discuss the questions.

- What is the man doing in the picture above?
- If the air-conditioner is broken in your hotel room, what should you do?
- What expertise is needed to be a hotel engineer?

Job Description

▶▶ Maintenance Service

- Control maintenance costs;
- Develop energy savings;
- Perform preventive maintenance;
- Maintain building interior;
- Make upkeep of building exterior.

Conversation

Conversation 1

Repairing an Air-conditioner

(Scene: John is calling the Housekeeping for the problem of the air-conditioner.)
(A= Anna, Housekeeper; J=John, Guest)

A: Anna from Housekeeping speaking. Can I help you?
J: I hope so. I'm very annoyed.
A: What's the problem, sir?
J: When I came back, I found the air-conditioner was leaking and the wall behind was wet. There's water all over the floor.
A: I guess the condenser is broken. That's really urgent.
J: Well, besides that, I can't get any cold air and it's like a steamer here. What should I do now?
A: Please turn off the air-conditioner now and which room are you in, sir?
J: Room 1208.
A: I'll inform the maintenance department right now Mr. Smith. They

New Words
annoy v. 惹恼,使人不悦
leak v. 漏,泄漏
condenser n. 冷凝器
inform v. 通知,告诉

will send someone up to fix it immediately.

J: Thank you for all your help.

fix *v.* 修理

Conversation 2

Repairing a TV Set

(Scene: Tom is repairing the TV set in a guest room.)
(T=Tom, Engineer; A= Alice, Guest)

T: Housekeeping. May I come in?

A: Come in, please.

T: The TV set is not working well, is it?

A: No, it isn't. I reported the problem to the floor attendant just now.

T: I'm here to check it. May I have a look at it?

A: Here it is. I think something is wrong with the colour and the reception. Besides, the picture is very fuzzy.

T: I see. I think the video tube is broken.

A: That's too bad. The Europe Cup is going to start. Can you fix it right now?

T: I'm afraid we have to send it back to the manufacturer, but we will get you a new TV set right away.

A: That's great!

T: Everything is OK now. Is there anything else I can do for you?

A: No, thanks! How efficient!

New Words

reception *n.* 接收效果
fuzzy *adj.* 模糊的,不清楚的
video tube 显像管
manufacturer *n.* 制造商
efficient *adj.* 有效率的

Conversation 3

Fixing the Toilet

(Scene: Susan is receiving a phone call from Alice who is reporting a problem of the toilet.)
(S= Susan, Housekeeper; A= Alice, Guest; M=Mark, Plumber)

S: Housekeeping. How can I help you?

酒店情境英语（上）

A: Yes, there seems to be something wrong with the toilet.

S: I am sorry to hear that. We'll send someone to repair it immediately. What's your room number, please?

A: Room 1288.

Five minutes later, the plumber Mark is knocking at the door of Room 1288.

M: Housekeeping. May I come in?

A: Come in, please.

M: What's the trouble, miss?

A: The toilet doesn't flush.

M: Let me see. Oh, it's blocked up...It is alright now. You may try it.

A: Yes, it's working now. Thank you.

M: You are welcome. Anything else?

A: The water tap drips all night long and the noise kept me awake all night.

M: Let me check. The joint part needs to be replaced. I will be back soon with a new one.

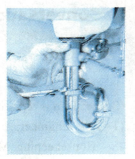

New Words

plumber *n.* 水管工人
flush *v.* 冲水
block *v.* 堵塞，塞住
tap *n.* 水龙头
drip *v.* 滴水
joint *adj.* 连接的

Useful Words and Expressions

drainage 下水道	Something has gone wrong with... ……坏了。
elevator 电梯	The alarm clock is not working. 闹钟坏了。
heating 暖气设备	The water is running all day. 水流了一天。
refrigerator 冰箱	I'll send an electrician to fix... 我会派一个电工去修理……
electrical system 电路系统	We'll have someone to fix it for you. 我们会派一个人去给您修理。
leaky faucet 漏水的水龙头	I'll ask the maid to change the drapes. 我会派一个客房服务员帮您更换窗帘。

◆ Unit 10 Maintenance Service

burst pipes 爆裂的水管

burnt fuses 烧掉的保险丝

blocked drains 堵塞的下水道

loose wires 线路松动

Some part needs to be replaced.
某个部件需要更换。

We apologize for the inconvenience.
对给您造成的不便我们深表歉意。

We guarantee that this won't happen again.
我们保证这种事情再也不会发生了。

I'm sorry but we can't fix it today.
很抱歉,今天修不好了。

Practical Form

Maintenance Request Form 维修申请单

ENGINEERING 工程部				
SERIAL NO. 申请单号	1128			
REQUESTED BY 申请人				
NAME 姓名		DEPARTMENT 部门	DATE 日期	20/02/2014
LOCATION 地点	Female Toilet 3 F4 四层第三个女厕所			
PRIORITY 优先权	Emergency critical to operation 影响运作,立即维修			
PROBLEMS 问题	Toilets are not working; liquid soap dispenser racks feel loose. 厕所马桶不工作;皂液架松动。			
ASSIGNED TO 维修人员				
TIME COMPLETED 完成修理时间				
DURATION 修理总时长	0 Hrs 30 Min. 30分钟			

酒店情境英语（上）

Maintenance Checklist 维护、维修一览表

ROOM#		DATE	NAME	
LIVING ROOM	Light & Switch 照明和开关	Door Surface 房门表面		
	Door Frame 门框	Door Closure 房门闭合情况		
	Ceiling Surfaces 天花板	Electrical Outlets 电源插座		
	Door Lock 门锁	Sink, Surface, Drain, Fixtures, Stopper 洗手盆、表面、排水、盆塞		
	Door Stop 门挡	Door Handle, Hinges 手柄，门枢		
	Security Latch 安全插销	Carpet, Seams & Stains 地毯、裂缝、污渍		
	Full-Length Mirror 全身镜	End Tables 茶几		
	Sofa 沙发	Ironing Board 熨衣板		
	Luggage Rack 行李架	Mini-bar 迷你吧		
BATHROOM	Marble Floor 大理石地板	Sink Surface 洗手盆表面		
	Exhaust Vent 排气口	Sink Drain 洗手盆排水		
	Towel Racks 毛巾架	Sink Stopper 洗手盆塞		
	Night Light 夜灯	Sink Piping 洗手盆管道		
	Tissue Fixture 厕纸架	Shower Door 淋浴门		
	Bath Tub Stopper 浴缸塞	Shower Drain 淋浴排水		
	Soap Dish 肥皂盒	Shower Head 淋浴喷头		
	Whirlpool 旋涡按摩浴池	Water Closet Operation 座便器情况		
	Water Pressure 水压	Water Closet Seat 马桶座圈		
	Cosmetic Mirror 梳妆镜	Hair Dryer 吹风机		

BEDROOM	Lounge Chair 躺椅	Desk Chairs 书桌椅
	Ottoman 长榻	Desk Drawer 书桌抽屉
	Armoire 壁橱	Desk Lamp & Shade 书桌台灯&灯罩
	Web TV Keyboard 网络电视键盘	Alarm Clock 闹钟
	Television 电视	Telephone 电话
	Remote Control 遥控器	Headboard 床头板
	Smoke Detector 烟感器	Nightstand 床头柜
	Floor Lamp & Shade 落地灯&灯罩	Safe 保险箱
	Drapes 窗帘	Bed 床
	Thermostat 恒温(调节)器	HVAC (heating, ventilation, air conditioner) 采暖通风与空调

Abbreviations and Technical Terms

SR: Standard Room 标准间	**SS:** Standard Single 标准单人间
ST: Standard Twin 标准双人间	**DR:** Double Room 双人间
TSU: Twin for Sole Use 标准间单人住	**SWB:** Single Room with Private Bath 带浴室单人房
DWB: Double Room with Private Bath 带浴室双人房(双人大床)间	**TWB:** Twin Beds Room with Private Bath 带浴室两人单人床房
King Size & Queen Size Room 大床间	Triple 三人间

Knowledge

Types of Maintenance

◆ Routine maintenance
◆ Preventive maintenance
◆ Emergency maintenance

Housekeeping and Maintenance

Despite all the routine and preventive maintenance efforts, emergencies still may occur in a hotel. For example, a toilet could be blocked or an air conditioner could stop working suddenly. Guests normally choose to report these situations directly to the Front Desk and the maintenance person on call will complete the work in a timely manner.

A successful maintenance program requires teamwork and cooperation with other departments including Front Desk and Housekeeping. Room attendants often take up initial maintenance functions for which Maintenance is ultimately responsible. Most minor repairs can be carried out while the room itself is being cleaned. Communication between the two departments should be efficient so that necessary repairs, adjustment or replacements can be performed in time.

Exercises

Speaking Practice

Activity 1: Discussion

Discuss with your partner about the functions of routine maintenance in a hotel.

◆ Unit 10 Maintenance Service

Activity 2: Role-play

Role-play 1

Guest: You are Mrs. Baker and you find that the thermostat in your room is broken. It is freezing in your room. So you call the Housekeeping to repair it.

Clerk: You are a housekeeping clerk. You apologize to Mrs. Baker and promise to send someone from the Maintenance Department to fix the thermostat.

Role-play 2

Guest: You are Mr. Smith calling the Housekeeping because there is power failure in your room.

Clerk: You are a housekeeping clerk. Answer the call and tell the guest that you will send an electrician right away.

Listening and Writing

Activity 1: Blank Filling—Handling Computer Problems

Listen and fill in the blanks.

C: Good morning. Service Center. Carol speaking. How may I help you?

S: Yes, I don't know why _____ suddenly. Would you please send someone to my room right now?

C: What is your room number, sir?

S: Room 1908.

C: Yes, Mr. Smith. I'll _____ the engineering immediately.

The engineer is knocking at the door of Room 1908.

T: Engineering. May I come in?

S: Yes, please.

T: What is the problem, Mr. Smith?

S: I was _____ the web, but suddenly it _____. I can't get it to work.

T: Let me have a look. Oh, the Internet access is not connected closely. Now try this, Mr. Smith.

S: Yes, it works. How can I turn to the homepage after _____?

T: Let me show you.

Activity 2: Writing Task

Write a letter to the maintenance engineers and ask them to carry out the Routine maintenance on the elevators in the hotel.

Activity 3: Translation

1. My toilet is stopped up.
2. I'll send for the plumber to fix it for you.
3. The alarm clock in my room is not working.
4. The faucet in my room cannot be turned on.
5. I'll send for an electrician from the Maintenance Department.

Unit 11   Special Service

Lead-in Activity

Look at the pictures and discuss the questions.

- What service do you think the attendant is offering?
- Have you ever asked for special services in the hotel?
- How to get the special services in the hotel?

Job Description

▶▶ **Special Service**

- Provide baby-sitting service;
- Provide shoe-shining service;
- Provide morning call service;
- Deal with lost and found;
- Deal with emergencies;
- Offer things at the guests' requests.

Conversation

Conversation 1

Buying Things on Request

(Scene: John is asking the housekeeper to buy him some traditional Beijing snacks for the friends' visit.)

(A= Anna, Housekeeper; J=John, Guest)

A: Good morning, sir. What can I do for you?

J: Some friends of ours are coming to town this evening. Would you please buy me some traditional Beijing snacks?

A: Sure. What kinds of snacks do you want?

J: I'm very interested in food that made of glutinous rice. Do you have any recommendations?

A: Well, how about Lv Da Gun and Ai Wo Wo? Both of them are made from glutinous rice and they are the most popular snacks here in Beijing.

J: Sounds great. Are there any differences between them?

New Words

glutinous *adj.* 黏的
snack *n.* 小吃,点心

A: Of course. Lv Da Gun is a rice cake filled with red peas, and then drizzled over with fried bean flour. Ai Wo Wo is shaped into a ball with walnut, sesame, melon seeds and sugar in it.

J: My mouth is already watering. I want a dozen for each.

A: No problem, sir. Do you need anything else? Like some flowers?

J: That's a good idea. Can you help me get some roses?

A: So snacks and a bouquet of roses, am I correct, sir?

J: That's right. Here is 500 *yuan* in advance.

A: Thank you, sir. I'll have them bought for you as soon as possible.

drizzle *v.* (在食物上)撒，淋
bouquet *n.* 花束

Conversation 2

Providing Baby-sitting Service

(Scene: Tom is asking Anna about the baby-sitting service provided in the hotel.)
(A= Anna, Housekeeper; T=Tom, Guest)

T: Hi. I'd like some information about your baby-sitting services.

A: OK, sir. We provide professional and reliable baby-sitting services trusted by parents for over 30 years. All the sitters here are experienced and responsible.

T: What is the charge then?

A: Our babysitting service charges 50 *yuan* per hour with a minimum of four hours.

T: Good. My wife and I are going to the concert hall tonight. I guess we need a babysitter to look after the two kids.

A: No problem, sir. At what time would you like the babysitter to come to your room?

T: We leave at 6 p.m., and please tell the babysitter to come before 6.

A: No problem. May I ask how old the children are?

T: My little girl is two years old, and the boy is five.

A: Two and five. Is there anything special you'd like the babysitter to do?

T: The babysitter should give them some milk and put them to bed before 10 p.m. And one more thing, my little girl still wears diapers. I'll leave some in the bag on the table.

New Words
baby-sit *v.* 代人临时照看婴儿
experienced *adj.* 有经验的
diaper *n.* 尿布

酒店情境英语（上）

Conversation 3

Dealing with Guest Injury

(Scene: Mr. Scott slipped on the corridor and called the housekeeping for help.)
(A= Anna, Housekeeper; S= Mr. Scott, Guest)

S: Hi. Room attendant, can you come here, please?

A: Yes, sir. What can I do for you?

S: I slipped in the tub during bath. I guess I sprained my left ankle as I can't move right now.

A: How unfortunate! Please don't move, Mr. Scott. I will be right there.

A few minutes later, the room attendant arrives.

A: Mr. Scott, just lean on me and I'll help you to bed.

S: Oh, my goodness! My left leg looks puffy. I hope that I haven't broken my leg.

A: Mr. Scott, I've asked the doctor to come. He will be right up and give you a thorough check.

S: My leg is fairly aching. It seems that I have to cancel my flight to Nanjing tonight.

A: I'm afraid so, Mr. Scott. Hope you can recover soon.

New Words

slip *v.* 滑倒
sprain *v.* 扭伤
puffy *adj.* 膨胀的，肿胀的
recover *v.* 恢复健康（体力、能力等）

Useful Words & Expressions

injure 受伤

bleed 流血

pinch 捏，掐

Can you get in touch with...
您能与……联系吗？

I'll send a confirmation form for you to sign.
我发给您一封确认函需要您签字。

The ankles are twisted.
踝关节扭伤了。

Unit 11 Special Service

fracture 骨折	Shall I send for a doctor? 要我派一位医生吗？
concussion 脑震荡	The in-house doctor will be in your room soon. 驻店医生马上就到您的房间。
cough 咳嗽	May I suggest you the baby-sitting service? 我为您推荐托婴服务。
itchy 痒	He has trouble with diarrhea. 他腹泻了。
sneeze 打喷嚏	I have a headache; I'm feeling nauseous; I feel like vomiting. 我感觉头疼，恶心想吐。
have a fever 发烧	He has a sore throat and a stuffy nose. 他嗓子疼，鼻子不通气。

Practical Form

Hotel Baby-sitting Registration Form 托婴服务登记表

ABC HOTEL CHILDCARE SERVICE

PARENTS' DETAILS 父母信息

Mother's Name: 母亲姓名：		Father's Name: 父亲姓名：	
Home Address: 家庭住址：			
Home Tel: 家庭固定电话：	Mobile No.: 手机号码：		E-mail: 电子邮箱：

HOTEL'S DETAILS 酒店信息

Hotel's Name: 酒店名称：	Room No.: 房号：
Address with Post Code: 酒店地址及邮编：	

酒店情境英语（上）

Hotel's Phone No.: 酒店电话：		Arrival Date: 抵店日期：		Departure Date: 离店日期：	

CHILREN'S DETAILS 孩子信息

Name 姓名	DOB 出生日期	Gender 性别		Allergies 过敏	
		☐ Boy/男	☐ Girl/女	☐ No/否	☐ Yes/是
		☐ Boy/男	☐ Girl 女	☐ No/否	☐ Yes/是
		☐ Boy/男	☐ Girl 女	☐ No/否	☐ Yes/是

Please give the details of any special needs or dietary requirements:
请提供其他特殊要求或者饮食需要：

Please give any other information you feel would be beneficial to the sitter:
请列出其他信息以供保姆参考：

☐ I have read and understand the terms and conditions of the ABC Hotel Children Care Service and agree to abide by them. 我已阅读ABC酒店托婴服务各项条款并同意遵守。

Signature 签名：

Date 日期: 15/03/2014

Unit 11 Special Service

Lost & Found Record Log 失物招领记录

LOST AND FOUND LOG

Date 日期	Guest Name 客人姓名	Room No. 房号	Article Items & Description 物品名称 描述	Finder 发现人	Handled by 经手人	Signature 签字

Abbreviations and Technical Terms

DS: Deluxe Suite 豪华套房	**BS:** Business Suite 商务套房
PS: Presidential Suite 总统套房	**ES:** Executive Suite 行政套房
IS: Imperial Suite 皇室套房	**PS:** Penthouse Suite 楼顶套房
Front View Room 朝街房	Rear View Room 背街房
City View room 城景房	Garden View Room 园景房
Sea View Room 海景房	Mountain View Room 山景房

Knowledge

Shoe-shine Service

- Set up shoe-shine station
- Greet the guest
- Start polishing the shoes
- Collect payment from the guests

The Diversity of the Roles of HK Department

While the hotel housekeeping department is commonly known for ensuring the tidiess of both public areas and guests' rooms—cleaning and dusting, replenishing supplies, as well as changing linens and bedding—the work duty for housekeeping staff extends beyond hotel cleanliness.

In modern properties, the housekeeping staff cooperates closely with many other departments which readily provide help in maintenance, baby-sitting, gardening, laundry service, bell service and floor management service, etc. Occasionally, it also gets help from customer service professionals to handle guests' requests.

Exercises

Speaking Practice

Activity 1: Discussion

Talk with your class and list the services and facilities that the housekeeping department of a modern hotel can provide as many as possible.

Activity 2: Role-play

Role-play 1

Guest: You are Mr. Baker and you lost your suitcase this morning. You are at the Lost and Found office and asking for help.

Clerk: You are a clerk working in the Lost and Found office. Ask Mr. Baker to describe the suitcase and help him find the lost item.

Role-play 2

Guest: You ask the floor attendant whether you can have a baby-sitter when you are out from 2:00 p.m. to 5:00 p.m.

Clerk: You promise to arrange it for the guest. Tell the guest that the charge is 30 *yuan* an hour for a minimum of 4 hours.

Listening and Writing

Activity 1: Blank Filling—Looking after the Sick

Listen and fill in the blanks.

T: Room Service. May I come in?

S: _____.

T: Good morning, Mr. Smith. Here is the medicine you have asked for. Please take two tablets before meal.

A: _____? Are you sure? I usually take medicine after meals.

T: I'm sure, sir. Here is the instruction.

A: _____. Yes, it is. I hope it can stop my stomach ache. Can you get me _____?

T: Here you are, sir. Take care. It's very hot.

A: I feel much better now. But I still feel nauseated.

T: I suggest you to get a detailed examination.

A: Can you send a doctor for me please?

T: Of course, sir. We have an in-house doctor who _____ whenever you need help.

A: That's great!

T: I'll connect the doctor for you right now.

Activity 2: Writing Task

Write a Lost & Found Notice according to Role-play 1.

Activity 3: Translation

1. Let me pinch your leg to stop the bleeding.
2. I just want some aspirin for stomachache.
3. We don't take care of children under 18 months.
4. I can't buy you the medicine. It's against the hotel regulations.
5. We charge 240 *yuan* for child care service by an hour, for a minimum of one hour.

Unit 12   Communicating with Staff

Lead-in Activity

Look at the pictures and discuss the questions.

- Which departments do you think are closely connected with Housekeeping?
- Many people think housekeeping is all about cleaning. What do you think?
- What trainings should Housekeeping provide to room attendants?

Job Description

▶▶ Executive Housekeeper

- Be responsible for housekeeping operations;
- Be responsible for the training and supervision of the cleaning personnel;
- Inspect the premises to ensure the physical area is maintained in a pristine and orderly fashion;
- Have a vast knowledge of how to best clean, maintain, and showcase a property;
- Have in-depth knowledge of cleaning and maintaining fine furniture and art as well as normal furnishings and accessories;
- Develop a schedule and standards of excellence that are expected to be closely followed by his staff.

Conversation

Conversation 1

Discussing Guest Complaints

(Scene: Sam is talking with Mary face-to-face about complaints concerning her work.)
(S=Sam, Floor Housekeeper; M=Mary, Room Attendant)

S: Mary, come in. I need to talk to you about something.
M: What's the problem?
S: Well, it's the guests' complaints about your work.
M: Oh, no. I'm always trying to do my best. What's wrong?

S: You are complained about the way you make the beds.
M: I'll manage to improve. Anything else?
S: The room wasn't vacuumed very well.
M: What's your suggestion?
S: You'll work with another room attendant for a week.
M: Great idea. I can learn from her.
S: I hope so. Our hotel has very high standards and we value guests' complaints.
M: I understand. Thank you very much for giving me another chance.

New Words
make the beds 铺床，叠被

Conversation 2

Discussing the Customer Service Questionnaire

(Scene: Greg is discussing with Amy about the Customer Service Questionnaire.)
(G=Greg, Housekeeping Manager; A=Amy, Floor Housekeeper)

G: Hi, Amy. Can you spare me a few minutes to talk about the questionnaire?
A: Yes, Greg. The feedback is interesting.
G: OK. So how are we doing?
A: Most guests feel they get good value for money.
G: That's great. What do they say about coming back?
A: Many of them say they will.
G: Excellent. Do we get any complaints?
A: Yes, mainly about the room service. They think the food is good, but the delivery is a little bit slow.
G: Oh, we need to give the feedback to the F&B Department and work together with them.
A: I will do this later. They also complained about the disco being too noisy.
G: So we need to make some adjustments there.
A: I agree.
G: And what about the responsiveness of our staff?

New Words
questionnaire n.（统计或调查用）问卷
feedback n. 反馈，反馈信息
adjustment n. 调整
responsiveness n. 反应，响应

酒店情境英语（上）

A: They say they are very friendly and helpful.
G: Excellent. I will bring this up at our next staff meeting.

> bring up 提出

Conversation 3

Cross-departmental Communication

(Scene: Sam is receiving a phone call from Amanda who notifies Housekeeping about guests' check in and out.)
(S= Sam, Floor Housekeeper; A= Amanda, Reservationist)

S: Sam from Housekeeping speaking. What can I do for you?
A: Hi, Sam. This is Amanda. Are you available now to go over the room allocation plan?
S: Sure. How is it?
A: I think we may run into problems with late check-outs.
S: Why's that?
A: Two of the rooms have early check-ins, 303 and 403.
S: Then we'll have to assign new rooms to those guests.
A: O.K. It's the same with 805 and 815, but those new guests don't arrive early.
S: But 805 and 815 are honeymoon suites. It takes longer to prepare.
A: Well, how about the suites on the 10th floor?
S: That'll be perfect. Then we'll have enough time to get them ready.
A: Great. Do you have anything else to discuss?
S: No. I'd better get to work.

New Words
run into 遭遇（困难等）
assign *v.* 分配
honeymoon *n.* 蜜月

Useful Words and Expressions

fluency 流畅,流利度

gesture 姿势,手势

I speak as a man of experience.
我以过来人的身份讲这些话。

Can I give you a piece of my word?
我可以给你提个建议吗？

Unit 12 Communicating with Staff

eye contact 目光交流

facial expression 面部表情

active listening 积极倾听

I need some professional advice.
我需要请教一下专业人士的高见。

Any suggestions? We're hungry for ideas.
有什么意见吗？我们渴求宝贵的意见。

You've got to suffer a little to be successful.
吃得苦中苦，方为人上人。

Practical Form

Employee Satisfaction Survey 员工满意度调查

Employee Satisfaction Survey 员工满意度调查	YES	NO
1. I look forward to going to work on Monday morning. 每周一早上我都期待着上班。		
2. I feel positive and up most of the time I am working. 在大部分工作时间中我都乐观向上。		
3. I have good friends at work. 工作中我有知心的朋友。		
4. I feel valued and appreciated at work. 工作中我能得到重视和欣赏。		
5. I feel free to do things the way I like at work. 工作中我可以按照自己喜欢的方式做事。		
6. I respect the work of my peers. 我尊重同事的工作。		
7. Creativity and innovation are supported. 创造和革新在工作中得到支持。		
8. I feel informed about what's going on. 我能及时了解到周围发生的事情。		
9. My manager cares about me as a person. 经理很关心我。		
10. I am fairly compensated. 我的收入比较合理。		

酒店情境英语（上）

Hotel Performance Report 酒店绩效报告

ABC Hotel Performance—10-Year History						
Year	Occupancy	Change	ADR	Change	RevPAR	Change
2001	67.9 %	---	$150.54	---	$10221	---
2001	68.1	0.3 %	137.30	(8.8) %	93.57	(8.4) %
2003	68.4	0.4	127.98	(6.8)	87.54	(6.4)
2004	70.7	3.4	136.01	6.3	96.17	9.9
2005	66.5	(5.9)	138.74	2.0	92.27	(4.0)
2006	58.9	(11.4)	13986	0.8	82.38	(10.7)
2007	55.6	(5.6)	14347	2.6	79.71	(3.2)
2008	61.4	10.4	14100	(1.7)	86.64	8.7
2009	60.6	(1.3)	127.27	(9.7)	77.07	(11.0)
2010	70.3	16.0	136.87	7.5	96.25	24.9

Abbreviations and Technical Terms

RD: Room Division 房务部
HSK: Housekeeping 客房部
S&M: Sales and Marketing 销售市场部
ENG.: Engineering 工程部
REC: Recreation Center 康体部
SEC: Security Department 保安部
ENT: Entertainment Department 娱乐部
FN: Financial Department 财务部
LOG: Logistic Department 后勤部
H&B: Hair and Beauty Department 美容、美发部
PA: Public Area 公共区域
DOS: Director of Sales 销售经理
DOR: Director of Rooms 客务部总监
FC: Financial Controller 财务总监

Knowledge

Main Barriers to Effective Communication

- Material or physical barrier
- Linguistic barrier
- Cultural barrier
- Emotional barrier

Tips for Effective Communication

Listen actively:	Demonstrate that you are listening by nodding, making eye contact and confirming what they have said.
Use "I" statements:	"I" statements allow you to take responsibility for how you feel and what you want.
Stay aware:	Think before you speak and avoid offending people. Talking over people and dominating conversations are both undesirable.
Emphasize:	Put yourself in the other person's shoes. Imagine how they feel and show your respect to their feelings and opinions.
Be humble:	Be true to and honest with yourself. Acknowledge both your strengths and weaknesses. Don't talk to people as if you are superior to them.
Speak appropriately:	Be aware of the company you are in and use language that is acceptable to them.

Exercises

Speaking Practice

Activity 1: Discussion

Many people think that Housekeeping jobs are tiring, and if given the chance to work in a hotel, Housekeeping would be the last choice. What's your point of view on housekeeping work and what can be learned through it?

Activity 2: Role-play

Role-play 1

Clerk 1: You are Mike, Housekeeping Manager, and want to call Nancy, Front Office Manager to discuss how to improve the corporation between the two departments.

Clerk 2: You are Nancy, Front Office Manager. You discuss with Mike how to corporate effectively and avoid misunderstandings and disputes.

Role-play 2

Clerk 1: You are May, Floor Supervisor, and want to talk with Jack, Floor Captain about a bed-making competition.

Clerk 2: You are Jack, Floor Captain. You discuss with May about a bed-making competition among room attendants. You talk about the purpose, procedure, awards and other issues related to the competition.

Listening and Writing

Activity 1: Blank Filling—Discussing the Regular Cleaning Schedule

Listen and fill in the blanks.

A: I've noticed that the hotel is very tidy and clean.
B: Thanks. We work very hard to keep it that way.
A: What are your secrets?
B: We have _____.

A: Do you inspect every area?
B: Yes, I do. My room attendants know I expect quality cleaning.
A: Housekeeping is a tough job. Do you have a lot of _____?
B: No, we don't. We hold weekly meetings to _____.
A: What usually do you do at these meetings?
B: We teach correct postures for cleaning. This prevents _____.
A: That's important. Do you rotate jobs?
B: Yes, we do. We find that _____.
A: I see you take your work very seriously.
B: Yes. I believe _____.

Activity 2: Writing Task

Write a newsletter about the bed-making competition (refer to Role-play 2).

Activity 3: Translation

1. Communication involves more than words.
2. Communication can either be direct or indirect.
3. It's very important to give employees feedback on their own performance.
4. To keep the workplace running smoothly, employees must be in sync with one another.
5. Sometimes, all a manager has to do is to lead by example and his employees will follow.

Unit 13 Reservation and Seating Guests

Lead-in Activity

Look at the pictures and discuss the questions.

- What is a hostess?
- How does a hostess seat guests?
- Would you like to work as a host or hostess?

Unit 13 Reservation and Seating Guests

Job Description

▶▶ **Hostess**

- Book, change, or cancel table reservations;
- Receive, register and escort the guests;
- Hold the waiting guests and present the menu;
- Thank guests and send them off.

Conversation

Conversation 1

Taking a Reservation

(Scene: John is making a reservation at home through a call.)
(A= Alice, Hostess; J=John, Guest)

A: Good morning! How may I help you?

J: I'd like to book a table at your restaurant.

A: Sure. For when?

J: Next Sunday evening, July 8, at 7:30.

A: How many people in your party?

J: Two. Me and my wife.

A: Ok. May I have your name and telephone number, please?

J: It's John Smith. My number is (010) 6566-8974.

A: Ok. You're all set. Is there anything else I can do for you?

J: Actually yes. We're celebrating a special occasion. It's our wedding anniversary.

A: Oh, how nice! In that case, I'll arrange a candlelit table with a rose for you.

New Words

occasion *n.* 场合
anniversary *n.* 周年纪念日
candlelit *adj.* 烛光的

酒店情境英语（上）

J: That's wonderful. Thank you very much!

A: My pleasure. So we will see you next Sunday evening, at 7:30?

J: Absolutely.

A: Thank you for calling us. Have a nice day.

Conversation 2

Seating Guests Without Reservation

(Scene: Alice is welcoming guests in the hostess station.)

(T=Tom, Guest; A= Alice, Hostess)

A: Good evening and welcome, sir. Do you have a reservation?

T: Not really. Is there a vacant table for two?

A: We are clearing up some tables now. Would you mind waiting in the lounge for a few minutes? We will inform you as soon as the table is ready.

T: Certainly. Let's go to the lounge then.

A few minutes later

A: I am sorry to have kept you waiting. Now your table is ready. Please follow me.

T: Ok. By the way, is there entertainment this evening?

A: Tonight we have a fabulous Chinese singer.

T: That's perfect. Oh, that table is near the stage, can we sit there?

A: I'm sorry, sir. That table has been reserved. But your table also has a good view.

T: Ok. That's good.

A: This is your table, please sit down. Would you like to start with a drink?

T: Sure. Two glasses of iced water, please.

New Words

hostess station 迎宾台
vacant *adj.* 空缺的，空闲的
lounge *n.* 休息室
fabulous *adj.* 极好的

Unit 13 Reservation and Seating Guests

Conversation 3

When the Restaurant Is Full

(Scene: Alice is receiving a guest in the hostess station.)
(S= Mr. Scott, Guest; A= Alice, Hostess)

A: Good afternoon. Welcome to our restaurant. Do you have a reservation?

S: No. I'm afraid not. Do you have any table available?

A: Hmmm. I'm afraid we're very full at the moment. It's the peak season, you know.

S: How long is the wait?

A: An hour, at least.

S: Oh, we want it sooner than that.

A: Would you mind trying a different restaurant? There's a pretty good one nearby.

S: That'll do. Thank you.

A: My pleasure. Hope we can serve you next time.

New Words
peak season 旺季

Useful Words and Expressions

shift 轮班   Let me check if we have any vacancy.
                我查查是否有空位。

layout 布局   Any special requirement?
                还有其他特别要求吗?

cuisine 烹饪   We can only keep your table till…
                我们只能保留您的桌子到……

specialty 特色菜 At what time can we expect you?
                您大概几点到?

sausage 香肠   Would you like a table in the hall or in a private room?
                您是在大厅用餐还是在包间里?

congee 粥   How many guests are coming?
                要来多少人?

酒店情境英语（上）

chafing dish 暖锅

brunch times 早午餐时段

waiting list 等待名单

wheelchair accessibility
无障碍环境

Where would you like to sit?
您想坐在哪儿？

I'll show you to your table.
我带您去您的桌子。

Would you mind waiting until it is free or would you prefer another table?
您是要等别人吃完还是换另一张桌子？

Would you mind sharing a table?
您介意共用一张桌子吗？

Practical Form

Table Reservation Form 餐位预订表

ABC Hotel Grill

Table Reservation Form 餐位预订表

Name 姓名：_____ No. of Guests 顾客编号：_____
Date 日期：_____ Time 时间：_____
Lunch 午餐☐ Dinner 晚餐☐

Special Occasion 场合：Business 商务☐   Birthday Party 生日聚会☐
Anniversary 周年庆典☐ Other 其他☐
Special Requests 特殊要求：_____
Telephone/Room Number 电话或房间号：_____
Confirmed 已确认：

ABC Hotel, 11 Tianyuan Road, Beijing, 100000

Unit 13 Reservation and Seating Guests

Menu 菜单

MENU 菜单

APPETIZERS 开胃菜

Breaded Shrimp 面包虾 $9
Oyster in Cream Sauce 鲜奶牡蛎汁 $11
Steamed Mussels 蒸贻贝 $10

Soups 汤

Soup of the Day 例汤 $7
Clam Chowder 蛤肉汤 $8

MAIN COURSE 主菜
Grill 烧烤

Barbecued Burger 烧烤汉堡 $12
Spare Ribs 排骨 $16
Filet Mignon 菲力牛排 $22
New York or T-Bone Steak
纽约牛排或 T 骨牛排 $18
Beef Tenderloin 牛里脊 $14

Fish 鱼菜

Catch of the Day 本日最鲜 $18

ABC Hotel Grill

Fresh Lobster 龙虾 $16
Atlantic Salmon 大西洋鲑鱼 $14

Salads 沙拉

Garden Salad 田园沙拉 $7
Chef's Salad 主厨特制沙拉 $9

Side Orders 配菜

Potatoes (baked, fried, mashed)
烤土豆、炸土豆、土豆泥 $5
Onion Rings 洋葱圈 $5
Corn on the Cob 煮玉米 $4

DESSERTS 甜点

Pies (apple, pecan, pumpkin)
苹果派、核桃派、南瓜派 $3
Cake (cheese, chocolate)
奶酪蛋糕、巧克力蛋糕 $3
Ice Cream 冰激凌 $2

Abbreviations and Technical Terms

Tableware	
table knife 餐刀	soup spoon 汤匙
fish knife 切鱼刀	dessert spoon 点心匙
butter knife 黄油刀	coffee spoon 咖啡勺
fruit knife 水果刀	tea spoon 茶匙
cake knife 蛋糕刀	water glass 水杯
fish fork 鱼叉	coffee cup 咖啡杯
dessert fork 点心叉	tea cup 茶杯
soup ladle 汤勺	egg cup 鸡蛋杯

Knowledge

Notes of Taking Reservations

◆ Ask the caller's name, telephone number, date and time;
◆ Find out the number of guests and occasion;
◆ Record details in diary and repeat reservation details;
◆ Take special requests.

Procedures of Seating Guests

Generally speaking, it is the host or hostess' responsibility to lead guests to the table. But in some restaurants, the responsibility lies with the captain and headwaiter. The procedures of seating guests are listed as follows:

Unit 13 Reservation and Seating Guests

◆ Welcome and greet the guests at the door with a smile.

◆ For guests without reservations, the host or hostess should make sure if there are vacant tables. If the guests should wait for the table, they should be informed of the waiting time.

◆ For guests with reservations, confirm the information and then escort them to their reserved table and seat them.

◆ When keeping the guests waiting for the tables, it is necessary to give apology and make sure that the guests will be informed as soon as there is a vacant table.

◆ While seating the guests who have been kept waiting, it is necessary to apologize so as to relieve their impatience and anger.

◆ Apply the "Ladies First" rule when helping the guests to take the seats.

◆ Help the guests to sit down gently.

Exercises

Speaking Practice

Activity 1: Discussion

What qualities are required to be a host or hostess?

Activity 2: Role-play

Role-play 1

Guest: You are Mrs. Smith and want to book a table for you and your husband to celebrate his birthday on Saturday evening, at 8:00.

Clerk: You are the reservationist who answers the phone. Ask Mrs. Smith questions regarding the name, telephone number, time, and special requirements.

Role-play 2

Guest: You are Mr. Black and want a table for four without a reservation.

Hostess: You are a hostess. You ask them to wait for a few minutes in the lounge and seat them when a table is ready.

酒店情境英语（上）

Listening and Writing

Activity 1: Blank Filling—Seating Guests

Listen and fill in the blanks.

H: Good evening, have you got a _____?

B: Yes. We've made a reservation for a table for three at 8:00 PM _____ the name of Mr. Black.

H: Just a minute, please. I'll check the reservation list. Yes, Mr. Black. We've been expecting you. _____, please. Would this table suit you?

B: Well, it's not too bad. But my wife wants to have a table _____.

H: I'm sorry, sir. All the window tables have been _____. Would you mind waiting for about 10 minutes?

B: We'd _____ wait. We'll be waiting in Room 1101. Please call us as soon as you are ready.

H: Yes. We'll be sure to call you, Mr. Black.

Ten minutes later

B: Good evening. Your window table is _____ now. Sorry to have kept you waiting, Mr. Black.

Activity 2: Writing Task

Write a reservation letter according to dialogue 1.

Activity 3: Translation

1. Is there a minimum charge for my table?
2. Would you like to make a reservation for another time?
3. A deposit of 10 *yuan* is required to secure your booking.
4. A 10% discount will be offered to those holding a VIP card issued by our restaurant.
5. All liquors brought in will be subject to a 30% service charge based on their market price.

Unit 14 Taking Orders

Lead-in Activity

Look at the pictures and discuss the questions.

- What are the waiters doing in the pictures?
- What does a waiter do if the guests do not know what to order?
- What kind of restaurant is regarded as a top restaurant?

Job Description

▶▶ Waiter/waitress:

- Present the menu;
- Introduce the dishes;
- Advise on customers' choice;
- Take orders.

Conversation

Conversation 1

Helping Order Dishes

(Scene: John is looking at the menu. Alice comes over to take orders.)

(A= Alice, Waitress; J=John, Guest)

A: Excuse me, sir. Are you ready to order?

J: Yes. But there are so many things on the menu that look fine. I don't know what to order.

A: Ok. Then let's start with appetizer. What appetizer would you like?

J: Is the Caesar salad all greens?

A: No, it comes with chicken breast.

J: That sounds delicious. I'll take that.

A: Ok. How about the soup?

J: Pumpkin soup is my favorite.

A: Good choice. Pumpkin soup is the most popular soup in our restaurant. What main course would you like to take?

New Words

appetizer *n.* 开胃食品
breast *n.* 胸脯

Unit 14 Taking Orders

J: I am having steak.

A: Ok. How would you like your steak done, rare, medium or well-done?

J: Medium, please.

A: Would you like vinaigrette or Thousand Island dressing?

J: Thousand Island, please, can we have the dressing on the side?

A: Sure. Then the dessert, sir?

J: I want a piece of cheese cake. And a cup of coffee. That's all.

A: Sure. You have ordered Caesar salad with Thousand Island dressing on the side, pumpkin soup, medium steak, a piece of cheese cake and a cup of coffee. Right?

J: Yes.

A: Ok, please wait a moment. I'll be back with your appetizer.

> vinaigrette *n.* 色拉调味汁
> Thousand Island dressing 千岛酱

Conversation 2

Chinese Food

(Scene: Tina is recommending Mr. Wilson Chinese food.)

(W= Mr. Wilson, Guest; T= Tina, Waitress)

T: What would you like to order, sir?

W: I'd like to try some Chinese food.

T: Have you had any Chinese food here before?

W: No, I haven't. I don't know anything about Chinese food.

T: We serve different styles of Chinese food here, but I'm not sure which one you prefer.

W: What's the difference?

T: Well. Cantonese food is rather light; Beijing food is heavy; and Sichuan dishes are spicy and hot. They all taste differently.

W: Really. Do you have something special?

T: I think the Roasted Crispy Chicken and Sliced Beef with Green and Red Pepper are quite special.

New Words

crispy *adj.* 酥脆的
slice *v.* 将……切成薄片
pepper *n.* 胡椒，辣椒

酒店情境英语（上）

W: All right, I'll have them.
T: What else would you like to order?
W: Let me see. I'd like beancurd with minced meat and chili.
T: Would you like some soup? The Sichuan hot and sour soup is very delicious.
W: Yes, please.
T: Would you like some rice to go with them?
W: Yes. Thank you.

beancurd *n.* 豆腐
mince *v.* 切碎

Conversation 3

Today's Special

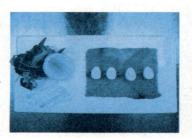

(Scene: Amanda is introducing today's special to Mrs. Scott who is looking at the lunch menu.)
(S= Mrs. Scott, Guest; A= Amanda, Waitress)

A: Good afternoon, my name is Amanda, and I'm your waitress today.
S: Nice to meet you, Amanda.
A: Are you ready to order from the lunch menu?
S: What a selection! But what should I choose?
A: Would you like me to introduce today's special?
S: Of course.
A: Today's special is business lunch special. It includes a starter, a main dish, a drink and a fortune cookie.
S: Thank you. I'll take it.
A: Ok. What beverage would you like?
S: A glass of cocktail, please.
A: Ok. Please wait a moment. I'll be right back.
S: Excuse me. What is this round tray in the middle of the table?
A: It's a lazy Susan. It spins around. So you can reach the different dishes.
S: That's wonderful.

New Words
fortune cookie 福饼, 喜饼
beverage *n.* 饮料
tray *n.* 托盘
lazy Susan 圆转盘
spin *v.* 旋转

Useful Words and Expressions

promotion 推销

ingredient 原料

allergy 过敏

rare 生的

squash 挤压

dessert 甜点

hors d'oeuvres 头盘

deep fried 炸得透

live entertainment 现场表演

a la carte 零点菜单

We offer special menus for different diets.
我们针对不同饮食提供专门的菜单。

Which flavor would you prefer, sweet or chili?
您喜欢哪种口味,甜的还是辣的?

It looks good, smells good and tastes good.
看起来很诱人,闻起来很香,吃起来很美味。

Would you like to put it on your hotel bill?
您是把它挂在酒店账上吗?

It is very popular with our guests. 它非常受客人欢迎。

It's served by the dozen. 按打卖。

It's out of season. 过季了。

It will stimulate the appetite. 它会刺激食欲。

This steak is too rare. I ordered it well-done.
这牛排太生了,我点的是全熟的。

Why not try our dinner buffet?
为什么不试试自助晚餐呢?

Practical Form

Promotion 促销广告

ABC INTERNATIONAL RESTAURANT

You won't regret an evening at ABC International Restaurant.

This international restaurant offers authentic food and live nightly entertainment. The music ranges from classical to traditional Italian and Mediterranean favorites.

Well-known chef put together a four-course dinner menu.
The menu includes favorite traditional French, Italian and Greek dishes. Choose between onion soup, gnocchi, caramel, lamb, kebabs, stuffed, vine leaves and more. The portions are generous, and the daily dessert special is fabulous.

A word of advice, call to find out when the Crème brûlée is being served. It's amazing.

Located at Tianyuan Road, Beijing 100000.

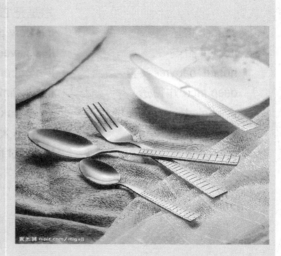

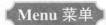

ABC INTERNATIONAL RESTAURANT

	BUSINESS LUNCH MENU 商务午餐 Price: $32 Thai, Korean, Japanese, and Chinese Specialties. Including: First course, main dish, beverage, and a fortune cookie. 泰国、韩国、日本和中国的特色菜。包括：头盘、主菜、饮料和甜点。	
	Thai 泰菜	Japanese 日本菜
First Course 头盘	Chicken or Beef Satay 鸡肉或牛肉沙嗲 Hot & Sour Lemongrass Soup 酸辣柠檬草汤	Sushi 寿司 Miso Shiru Soup 味增汤
Main Dish 主食	Pad Thai Noodles with Chicken or Beef 泰式鸡肉或牛肉面 Thai Fish Cakes 泰式鱼饼 Black Bean Chicken 豆豉鸡	Shrimp and Vegetable Tempura 蔬菜天妇罗 Beef or Chicken Teriyaki 照烧牛/鸡肉 Tofu with Japanese Sauce 日本豆腐
	Korean 韩国菜	Chinese 中国菜
First Course 头盘	Fried Prawns with Spicy Bean Sprouts 辛辣豆芽大虾汤 Ginseng Chicken Soup 人参鸡汤	Dim Sum(2 portions) 点心2份 Wanton Soup 云吞汤
Main Dish 主食	Spicy Fried Pork & Kimchee Noodles 椒盐猪肉和泡菜面条 Mixed Vegetables & Fried Rice 混合蔬菜和炒饭 Grilled Beef, Chicken, or Seafood 烤牛肉、鸡肉或海鲜	Crispy Lemon Chicken 香酥柠檬鸡 Half Peking Duck 半只北京烤鸭 Seafood Chop Suey 海鲜杂碎汤

Abbreviations and Technical Terms

Condiments	
ketchup 番茄酱	red vinegar 红醋
shrimp sauce 虾酱	aromatic vinegar 香醋
butter sauce 奶油酱	white vinegar 白醋
fish paste 鱼酱	edible oil 食用油
chutney 酸辣酱	soybean oil 豆油
mayonnaise 蛋黄酱	peanut oil 花生油
soybean pasta 豆瓣酱	olive oil 橄榄油

Knowledge

Service Types of Western Food

- French-style service 法式服务
- British-style service 英式服务
- American-style service 美式服务
- Russian-style service 俄式服务

Table Manners in Foreign Countries

  In America, don't empty a bottle into someone's glass, or else that person has to buy the next bottle. It's polite to put the last drops into your own glass.

  In France, never discuss money or religion over dinner. For French people, a meal is like a ceremony. People relish it and treat it like a special occasion. When they eat bread, they cut it on the tablecloth rather than on a plate. Before eating they tear it into bite-sized pieces. It is very impolite to take a bite from the whole piece.

In Japan, when you eat noodles, slurping mildly is not rude but is a compliment to the chef. Japanese people say it tastes better if you slurp.

Exercises

Speaking Practice

Activity 1: Discussion

Chinese food and western food, which one do you prefer? What are the differences between them?

Activity 2: Role-play

Role-play 1

Guest: Mrs. Baker and her three friends order only one soup and one vegetable.
Waiter: You are a waiter. You help them to order more dishes.

Role-play 2

Guest: You would like to have a sandwich. You want to know if it comes with chips. You want to know if they have got any mushrooms. Your second choice is a small salad. You would also like tomato juice.
Waiter: Ask what the diner would like. Ask if he would like anything else with the sandwich. It's served with chips. You're running out of mushroom. Ask if the guest wants something to drink.

Listening and Writing

Activity 1: Blank Filling—Taking an Order

Listen and fill in the blanks.

W: Here is your drink. Are you ready to order?
G: Yes, for an _____, we'd like to try the steamed mussels.

W: _____. The mussels come in a white wine sauce.
G: That sounds delicious.
W: And what would you like for your _____?
G: I'll try the beef tenderloin; and my wife will have the filet mignon.
W: Ok. How would you like it _____?
G: I'd like mine _____. And the filet mignon well done.
W: Would you like your steak with a baked potato or French fries?
G: We would _____ a baked potato, please.
W: What kind of salad would you like? A mixed salad or a tomato salad?
G: A mixed salad would be fine.
W: And what would you like to _____ with your meal?
G: I'd like to order wine.

Activity 2: Writing Task

Write an article to promote a dish.

Activity 3: Translation

1. Do you have any coupon with you?
2. What is your discounted course today?
3. Would you like to try our house special fried cod?
4. The price of five glasses of juice is equal to that of one jug.
5. Steamed pork wrapped with rice flour is our house special.

Unit 15 Serving Dishes

Lead-in Activity

Look at the pictures and discuss the questions.

- Where do the girls in the pictures work?
- What are their responsibilities?
- As a server, how do you satisfy the guests?

酒店情境英语（上）

Job Description

▶▶ Server:

- Serve, explain and change dishes;
- Clean tables;
- Deal with complaints.

Conversation

Conversation 1

Service during the Meal

(Scene: Jane is having dinner at the restaurant. Alan is serving him.)
(A= Alan, Waiter; J=Jane, Guest)

A: Are you enjoying your meal, madam?
J: I am indeed. Everything is delicious.
A: I'm glad to hear that. Is there anything else I can get you?
J: Yes, an orange juice, please.
A: Ok. Your bread basket is empty. Can I fill it for you?
J: Yes. Those rolls were fantastic. I want more.
A: Great. Can I clear away some of the plates?
J: Please take these three.
A: Perhaps another napkin? Eating ribs can be messy.
J: Yes, please. I just have to eat them with my fingers.
A: You're right. It's really a finger dish.
J: Good ribs are one of my favorite foods.
A: Please enjoy them. I'll be right back with everything.

New Words

roll *n.* 面包卷
fantastic *adj.* 极好的
napkin *n.* 餐巾纸
rib *n.* 排骨

Conversation 2

Following up with Guests

(Scene: Adam is serving guests at a restaurant.)
(T=Tom, Guest; A= Adam, Waiter)

A: How is your meal, sir?
T: Not very good. The minestrone soup was ok, but my lamb kabob is a little bit raw.
A: I am sorry to hear that, sir. Let me take it back to the kitchen and put it on the grill. How would you like it?
T: I don't like it rare. Make sure it's medium, please.
A: Ok. And how is the cheese salad?
T: Excellent. It is delicious.
A: I'm glad to hear that. And how are the rest of the entrées?
T: My girlfriend likes the cream sauce on the ravioli.
A: Great. Would you like some more drink?
T: Yes, a glass of apple juice, please.
A: Anything else?
T: No, I think that's enough.
A: Ok. I'll be right back with your juice.

New Words

minestrone n. 蔬菜通心粉汤
lamb n. 羔羊肉
kabob n. 烤肉串
grill n. 烤架
entrée n. 主菜或主菜前小菜
ravioli n. （意）略有馅的水饺

Conversation 3

Suggesting Wines

(Scene: Adam is recommending wines to Mr. Scott who is having dinner.)
(S= Mr. Scott, Guest; A= Adam, Waiter)

A: Good evening. Are you ready to order from the wine menu?
S: Not yet, I need your help on this. We'd like the right wine for

酒店情境英语（上）

each course.

A: Ok. What are your starters?

S: We ordered the steamed mussels and the breaded shrimp.

A: Sea food goes well with white wine. I suggest a Spanish Chardonnay.

S: Ok, I will take it. For the main course we ordered lobster and filet mignon.

A: Well, steak goes better with a full-bodied red wine.

S: Yes. But lobster goes better with a crisp white wine.

A: I recommend Cabernet Sauvignon. I think you'll both enjoy it.

S: Ok. We'll take the Cabernet Sauvignon for the main course.

New Words

mussel *n.* 蚌，贻贝
shrimp *n.* 小虾
Chardonnay *n.* 一种白葡萄酒
lobster *n.* 龙虾
filet mignon 无骨高档牛排

Useful Words and Expressions

greasy 油腻的	May I serve it to you now? 现在可以为您上菜吗？
stew 炖	This is the complete course. If you would like any additional dishes, please call me. 这是您点的所有的菜。如果您还想点其他的，请叫我。
congee 粥	We are full now. Can you cancel the soup, please? 我们吃饱了，能帮我们把汤退掉吗？
nutritious 有营养的	I'll check with the chef right now. 我马上去厨师那查一下。
chilled 冷冻的	That would be on the house. 那些是免费的。
seasoning 调味品	Would you like an aperitif with your meal? 您需要开胃酒配您的饭吗？
home style 自制	Would you like your rice now or later? 您是现在上米饭还是等会儿？
dim sum 点心	Your meal will be ready soon. 您的饭菜很快就好。
discount price 折扣价	I strongly recommend... 我强烈向您推荐……
hot pot 火锅	Would you like to start with... 您想以……开始吗？

Unit 15 Serving Dishes

Practical Form

Application Form 申请表

ABC INTERNATIONAL RESTAURANT

Application for Hotel Outlet
酒店餐厅消费申请

Request by 申请人：_____
Department 部门：_____
Position 职位：_____
Date of Application 申请日期：_____

Outlet name applied for 申请餐厅：

- ☐ Loong Yuen Restaurant 龙苑中餐厅
- ☐ Cafe Berlin 咖啡柏林西餐厅
- ☐ Paulaner 普拉那啤酒坊餐厅
- ☐ Marco Polo Trattoria 马可波罗意大利轻食坊
- ☐ Marco Polo Restaurant 马可波罗意大利餐厅
- ☐ Sky Lounge 空中酒廊
- ☐ Lobby Lounge 大堂酒廊
- ☐ ABC Deli ABC酒店美食廊

Others(其他)：

Reserved Outlet 预订餐厅名称：_____   Reserved by 预订接收人：_____
Estimated Pax 预订人数：_____   Event Time 用餐时间：_____

Applicant by(Signature & Date)：_____   Applicant's HOD(Signature & Date)：_____
申请人（签名及日期）   部门总监/经理（签名及日期）

Menu 菜单

ABC International

Dinner Menu $40 晚餐40美元

Traditional Soups 传统汤类
Italian Minestrone Soup 意大利蔬菜汤
Mediterranean Lentil Soup 地中海扁豆汤

Hors D'oeuvres 餐前菜
Cheese souffle served with a Waldorf salad
芝士蛋奶酥
Stuffed vine leaves with mincemeat, rice & herbs
葡萄叶饭卷

Entrees 主菜
French Classics 法国经典
Chef's Special: fresh fish or seafood
主厨特色菜
Veal escalope served with wild rice
小牛排配饭
Italian Classics 意式经典
Ravioli served in a cream sauce 意大利方饺
Fettuccine with grilled chicken and green onions
意大利宽面
Mediterranean Classics 地中海经典
Calamari—deep fried squid with rice 烤鱿鱼
Lamb Kabab—grilled lamb with roasted potatoes
羊肉串

Desserts 甜点
Make your choice from dessert cart
从甜点菜单选

Unit 15 Serving Dishes

Abbreviations and Technical Terms

Cooking Glossary	
steam 蒸	stew 焖
fry 油炸	smoked 熏的
grill 烤	salted 盐腌的
toast 烧烤	steeped 浸泡的
bake 烘焙	carved 切好的

Knowledge

Orders of Serving Dishes

- Starter or appetizer
- Soup
- Main course
- Dessert
- Coffee or tea

Tips of Good Service

Good service is more than just serving food. Check on your customers during the meal.
Remember to ask:
- Are you enjoying your meal?
- Is everything satisfactory?

Pay attention to the table:
- Are there plates you can clear?
- Is the bread basket empty?

◆ Should you fill the water glasses?
◆ Do they need another napkin?

If there are problems:
◆ If the meat is undercooked, take it back to the grill.
◆ If the vegetables are too salty, exchange them.
◆ Always offer to fix the problem.

Never keep your customers waiting:
◆ Tell your customers you will be back soon and return to them quickly.

Exercises

Speaking Practice

Activity 1: Discussion

Discuss with your partner how to decorate your restaurant and design a special menu on Valentine's Day to appeal to more guests.

Activity 2: Role-play

Role-play 1

Guest: You want a la carte. And ask for specialties.
Waiter: Give the specialties. And suggest wines and fruit.

Role-play 2

Guest: This is your first time to have Chinese food. You are asking some questions about Chinese food.
Waiter: Explain to the guest as best as you can.

Unit 15 Serving Dishes

Listening and Writing

Activity 1: Blank Filling—Dealing with Misserving

Listen and fill in the blanks.

G: Excuse me, sir. I ordered the hairy crab but you gave me the _____.

W: I'm awfully sorry, sir. There must be some mistake. I do _____ for giving you the wrong dish.

G: Can you change it?

W: Sure. The crab will take _____ to prepare. Would you like to take some complimentary drink while waiting?

G: I'm afraid I don't have enough time to wait for the next crab. I _____ at 7:00 in my room. Now it's 6:50.

W: Oh, you are staying at our hotel, sir?

G: Right. Room _____.

W: In this case, I shall ask the _____ to serve you a snack at 9:30 tonight, and you'll have your favourite hairy crab. It's _____.

G: That's good. Thank you.

W: Thank you for telling us. I assure you it _____. Please take your time and enjoy yourself.

Activity 2: Writing Task

You need to handle some personal matters. Write your manager a note asking for a leave of absence.

Activity 3: Translation

1. Would you bring us some toothpicks?
2. May I move the remaining meat to a smaller plate?
3. There is a free public phone a few steps from the room to the right.
4. Excuse me, sir. Would you mind moving to the side some so I can serve the soup?
5. All dips and sauces are here. They are vinegar, soy sauce, chili sauce, garlic paste and white pepper powder.

Unit 16 Room Service

Lead-in Activity

Look at the pictures and discuss the questions.

- Have you ever experienced room service?
- Why is room service always located inside the kitchen?
- What qualities are needed to work in this position?

Unit 16 Room Service

Job Description

▶▶ Room Service:

- Deliver food and beverage;
- Serve meals to guests in their rooms;
- Manage the mini-bar;
- Clear away the tray;
- Receive the bill.

Conversation

Conversation 1

Taking a Breakfast Order

(Scene: Mary is answering a phone call from a guest.)
(M= Mary, Waiter; J=John, Guest)

M: Room service. Mary is speaking. How may I help you?
J: This is Room 1920. I'd like to have breakfast in my room.
M: Sure, sir. What would you like to order?
J: I'd like the all American Breakfast.
M: How would you like your eggs, scrambled, over hard, over easy or sunny side up?
J: Sunny side up, please.
M: Fine. Ham, bacon, sausage, which one would you like?
J: Ham, please.
M: Toast or English muffin?
J: I prefer whole wheat toast.
M: Ok. Would you like tea or coffee?

New Words

scrambled egg 炒鸡蛋
over hard 煎全熟蛋
sunny side up 单面煎蛋
muffin n. 小松饼

酒店情境英语（上）

J: Coffee, please, decaf.

M: Let me say it back to you. Sunny side up eggs, ham, wheat toast and a pot of decaffeinated coffee. Is that all right?

J: Yes, that's right. I'd like my breakfast at 8:30 a.m.

M: Fine. Your order will be delivered hot, fresh, and on time.

> decaffeinated *adj.* 脱去咖啡因的

Conversation 2

Sending the Ordered Food

(Scene: Mark is sending dinner to a guest's room.)
(T=Tom, Guest; M= Mark, Waiter)

M: Room Service. May I come in?

T: Yes, please.

M: Good afternoon, sir. I've brought the dinner you ordered. Where would you like me to put them?

T: Just put them on the table. Over there.

M: Ok. Here are your appetizer, spicy bean sprout, fruit salad, fried pawn, fried pork, and consommé. Is that right?

T: Yes.

M: Here is the napkin. Let me place it.

T: No, thanks. I can do it myself.

M: Would you like anything else, sir?

T: Uh, please bring me a cheesecake and a cup of tea half an hour later.

M: Ok. here is the bill. How would you like to pay, in cash now or sign the bill?

T: I'll sign the bill and settle it when I check out.

M: Ok. I'll be back with the cake and tea in half an hour. Enjoy your meal, sir.

New Words

bean sprout 豆芽
consommé *n.* 清炖肉汤

Conversation 3

Service Charge

(Scene: Mark is presenting the bill to the guest.)
(S= Scott, Guest; M= Mark, Waiter)

M: Here is your bill, sir. I've really enjoyed serving you tonight.
S: We enjoyed ourselves, too. Your service was great.
M: Thank you very much. Would you like me to explain the bill to you?
S: Yes, please.
M: Rice porridge, 20 yuan. Pickles, 10 yuan. A preserved egg, 15 yuan. And steamed dumplings, 30 yuan.
S: I'm thinking there's a mistake. I didn't order the preserved egg.
M: Let me check. You're right, sir. Sorry about that.
S: What's the total now?
M: 66 yuan including the service charge.
S: OK.
M: Would you like to pay now or charge it to your room?
S: I'll pay you cash now, and I have a restaurant discount card.
M: Very good. Then you'll get a 10% discount off the meal.
S: Wonderful. Does the total include tax?
M: Yes, and tipping is at your discretionary.

New Words
rice porridge 大米粥
pickle *n.* 腌菜，泡菜
preserved egg 皮蛋，松花蛋
discretionary *adj.* 自由决定的

Useful Words and Expressions

manual 手工的   Room service is available 24 hours a day.
送餐服务全天为您开放。

exterior 外部的   There is an extra service charge of 15% for room service.
送餐服务要收15%的服务费。

hallway 走廊   We have a good choice of drinks.
饮料有很多选择。

酒店情境英语（上）

vanilla 香草 — Would you like ham or bacon with your eggs?
您是要火腿还是烤肉搭配您的鸡蛋？

tray 托盘 — Could I put your breakfast on the table?
我能把您的早餐放在桌子上吗？

cereal 谷物 — If you'd like to have your meals in the room, just dial room service.
如果您想在房间用餐，请打送餐服务电话。

hanger 衣架 — You may use a meal voucher for room service.
在房里用餐您可以用优惠券。

mineral water 矿泉水 — Thanks very much for the great service.
非常感谢这么好的服务。

delivery time 送达时间 — We can get that to you in about 10 minutes.
10分钟之内为您送到。

call down 责骂 — That will be... with tax.
加上税，一共是……

Practical Form

Lunch Menu 午餐菜单

Room Service 送餐服务

<u>Lunch at the ABC Hotel 午餐</u>
Ask us for delicious, creative options or special requests; non-dairy vegan or low-sugar. 我们为您提供美味食物，满足您的要求，如素食或低糖。

<u>Available 营业时间：</u>
11:30 a.m.—2:00 p.m.(Monday—Friday);
12:00 p.m.—2:30 p.m.(Saturday and Sunday)

MENU 菜单

<u>Classic Stew 经典炖汤</u>
Beef stew with carrots and green beans served on a bed of egg noodles. 烩牛肉配鸡蛋面
Salad served with your choice of dressing 沙拉（调料自选）

<u>From the Sea 海鲜</u>
Catch on the day served with baked potato of French fries. 今日特鲜配薯条
Mediterranean salad served with your choice of dressing. 地中海沙拉（调料自选）

<u>Vegetarian Special 素食</u>
Vegetarian chili-mild to spicy according to taste served on a bed of rice. 素菜配米饭
Your choice of steamed vegetables. 自选蔬菜

Unit 16 Room Service

Breakfast Menu 早餐菜单

Room Service 送餐服务

Breakfast at the ABC Hotel 早餐

We are pleased to deliver your order hot, fresh and on time. 我们竭诚为您送上刚出锅的、热腾腾的饭菜。

Available 营业时间：

6:30 a.m.—11:00 a.m.(Monday—Friday);
早上6:30——中午11:00(周一至周五);

7:00 p.m.—11:00 a.m.(Saturday and Sunday)
早上7:00——中午11:00 (周六和周日)

MENU 菜单

All American Breakfast 美式早餐

Two eggs-scrambled, omelet or sunny side up.
两个炒鸡蛋、煎蛋卷或单面煎蛋

Choice of ham, bacon or sausage.
任选火腿、培根或火腿肠

Toast or English muffin. 土司或英式松饼

From the Griddle 煎制品

Pancakes or waffles 煎饼或华夫饼

Choice of ham bacon or sausage
任选火腿、培根或火腿肠

Orange or grapefruit juice 橙汁或葡萄汁

Baked Items 烤制品

Danish Pastry 丹麦糕点

Croissant 羊角面包

Corn muffin 玉米松饼

Beverage 饮料

Pot of tea—regular or decaffeinated 一壶茶
（普通的或去咖啡因的）

Pot of coffee—regular or decaffeinated
一壶咖啡（普通的或去咖啡因的）

Hot chocolate 热巧克力

Abbreviations and Technical Terms

Tableware

silverware 银器	mustard pot 芥末罐
sugar bowl 糖罐	China spoon 瓷勺
sugar tongs 方糖夹子	toothpick 牙签
milk jug 奶罐	ashtray 烟灰缸
caster 调味品瓶	percolator 煮咖啡壶

Knowledge

Types of Breakfast

American Breakfast

Continental Breakfast

Chinese Breakfast

Japanese Breakfast

Unit 16 Room Service

Room Service

In general three-star hotels or above provide room service. That is, guests can have their meals inside their rooms. Room service belongs to the Food and Beverage department instead of Housekeeping. Room service is responsible for serveing beverages in the rooms and manage the mini-bar after the hotel bar closes. Guests' food should be delivered fresh, hot and on time, so the room service is often located inside the kitchen and close to the service elevator. A tray or a rolling table is used for the dishes. Each dish is covered during delivery and uncovered upon entering the room.

When the guests have finished their meal, room service usually clears away the tray in two ways: one is by asking the guests to place the tray outside of the room after they finish. The other is by asking the guests to call them to come and collect the tray.

Exercises

Speaking Practice

Activity 1: Discussion

How can a waiter in room service become the Director of F&B?

Activity 2: Role-play

Role-play 1

Guest: You are calling room service for a steak, some drinks and some dessert. You want to have them around 11:30 a.m.

Waiter: You are to handle this order and you know the room number, the food, when to deliver, etc.

Role-play 2

Guest: You have ordered a glass of apple juice, two boiled eggs, some sandwiches and a cup of tea for breakfast.

Waiter: You deliver the ordered food to the guest and ask the guest to pay the bill.

酒店情境英语（上）

Listening and Writing

Activity 1: Blank Filling—Offering Room Service
Listen and fill in the blanks.

W: Good morning, _____. May I help you?
G: I'd like to have breakfast in the room.
W: Certainly, madam. What would you like to order?
G: I'd like a _____, two boiled eggs and some toast.
W: How long would you like your eggs boiled, madam?
G: _____ is enough, I think.
W: Would you like some tea or coffee, madam?
G: I'd like a cup of coffee with _____.
W: Yes, madam. Is there anything else you want?
G: No, thanks.
W: I'll repeat your order. One fresh orange juice, _____, toast and a cup of coffee with fresh milk. Is that all right, madam?
G: That's correct.
W: May I have your name and room number?
G: Yes. _____. Mrs. Johnson.
W: Your order will be ready in 20 minutes. See you then.

Activity 2: Writing Task
Write a letter to your manager for better management in room service.

Activity 3: Translation
1. It's our house special.
2. The wine list is on the last page of the menu.
3. It is 550 *yuan*, and the 15% service charge is included.
4. You can place the items in the corridor outside your room.
5. Let me place your napkin here, so you can face the TV and watch the news.

练习参考答案

Unit 1

Activity 1: Blank Filling

1. A heavy fog 2. depends on 3. transport service 4. takes off 5. meeting room

Activity 3: Translation

1. 我打电话来是想预订一间总统套房。
2. 请将这六间房都预订在Ray的名下。
3. 我们是通过传真还是邮件的形式确认预订?
4. 给您带来不便,深感抱歉。
5. 我们可以给您提供每晚1000元的特价。

Unit 2

Activity 1: Blank Filling

1. too noisy 2. lovely view 3. room changing form 4. send a bellboy up
5. sound sleep

Activity 3: Translation

1. 您可以接受吗?
2. 真遗憾您的航班延误了。
3. 这是您的早餐券。
4. 如果我在这里待上一阵子会有折扣吗?
5. 我们将免费给您升级到豪华套房。

Unit 3

Activity 1: Blank Filling
1. We Rent Cars   2. driver's license   3. 500 *yuan*   4. deposit   5. arrange

Activity 3: Translation
1. 请给我在明早8点安排一辆出租车。
2. 你知道去哪儿买纪念品比较好吗?
3. 我建议您徒步游览这座城市。
4. 纪念馆很值得一去。
5. 请您在领取行李时出示这张领取卡。

Unit 4

Activity 1: Blank Filling
1. 021-64538502   2. private number   3. Shanghai International Advertising Company
4. extension   5. hang up

Activity 3: Translation
1. 我会再核对一下电话号码。
2. 我想打个电话到悉尼。
3. 请问我该怎么拨打外线电话?
4. 我们挂断电话再重打一次吧?
5. 他房间电话的话筒没放好。

Unit 5

Activity 1: Blank Filling
1. prices for renting facilities   2. Here is the rate list.   3. slide projector
4. get a 10% discount   5. H0543683   6. by 9:00 am

Activity 3: Translation
1. 会议室的租金是按半天计算的,每间2500元。

2. 请用您的房卡号码连接到我们的无线网络。
3. 我们会将复印件送到您的房间。
4. 您是想要头等舱还是经济舱呢?
5. 我们不能使用客人的储存卡。

Unit 6

Activity 1: Blank Filling
1. toilet   2. clogged   3. Mr. White   4. Maintenance Service
5. we fix it while you are not in the room   6. apologize for the inconvenience

Activity 3: Translation
1. 我想向你们经理投诉。
2. 我们保证下次首先收拾您的房间。
3. 这件毛衣洗坏了,你们的服务太差了。
4. 如果您还需要其他服务,请联系我们。
5. 隔壁房间太吵了,弄得我头痛。

Unit 7

Activity 1: Blank Filling
1. check out   2. here is my room card.   3. I'm getting your bill ready
4. comes to 3850 *yuan*   5. deposit receipt   6. keep the invoice

Activity 3: Translation
1. 我们会把剩余的钱款返还给您。
2. 第五项是对您的洗衣服务的收费。
3. 我们接受美国运通卡、万事达卡和维萨卡付款。
4. 您能检查一下账单是否有错误吗?
5. 如果您是下午6点之后退房,您需要支付全天的费用。

Unit 8

Activity 1: Blank Filling

1. How may I help you?   2. What can I do for you?   3. front desk
4. leave a note to the overnight shift   5. have your name and room number, please
6. It's my pleasure, Mr. Graham.

Activity 3: Translation

1. 我们总是优先打扫有服务请求的房间。
2. 您什么时候方便?
3. 我要扫一下桌子上的灰尘,我是否可以移动您桌子上的物品?
4. 您能否把冰箱里的啤酒和烈酒撤走?
5. 您需要客房清理服务的时候请给前台打电话。

Unit 9

Activity 1: Blank Filling

1. dry cleaning   2. removed   3. send a valet to come up   4. pick up
5. check the laundry form

Activity 3: Translation

1. 我的衬衣掉了几粒扣子。
2. 这件毛衣要冷水手洗。
3. 我确实需要一个熨斗和一个熨衣板来熨衣服。
4. 我们尽力去除污渍但是不能保证结果。
5. 快洗服务或者熨烫需要另加50%的费用。

Unit 10

Activity 1: Blank Filling

1. the computer stopped working   2. contact with   3. logging on   4. crashed   5. surfing

Activity 3: Translation
1. 厕所堵了。
2. 我派一位管道工人帮您修一下。
3. 我房间的闹钟坏了。
4. 我房间的水龙头打不开了。
5. 我从维修部派一位电工。

Unit 11

Activity 1: Blank Filling
1. Come in, please. 2. Before meal 3. Let me take a look at it. 4. some hot water
5. is available

Activity 3: Translation
1. 我帮您捏着腿止血。
2. 我想要一点儿阿司匹林止胃痛。
3. 托婴服务不包括小于18个月的婴儿。
4. 我不能为您买药，这是违反酒店规定的。
5. 托婴服务每小时收费240元，最少一个小时。

Unit 12

Activity 1: Blank Filling
1. a regular cleaning schedule with constant inspections 2. staff turnover
3. motivate our staff 4. staff injuries 5. job rotation prevents staff boredom
6. hotel cleanliness is a big part of customer satisfaction

Activity 3: Translation
1. 交流不只是语言的沟通。
2. 交流可以是直接的，也可以是间接的。
3. 对员工的表现给予反馈非常重要。
4. 要使工作环境顺畅，员工之间必须和睦相处。
5. 有时，管理者要做的就是以身作则，这样员工就会服从。

Unit 13

Activity 1: Blank Filling
1. reservation 2. under 3. Step this way 4. by the window 5. reserved 6. better
7. ready

Activity 3: Translation
1. 我们订的桌位有没有最低消费？
2. 您能换到其他预订时间吗？
3. 我们要收取10元订金来确保您的预订。
4. 有贵宾卡可以享有九折优惠。
5. 自带酒水会按该酒市场价格的30%作为服务费。

Unit 14

Activity 1: Blank Filling
1. appetizer 2. Good choice 3. main course 4. cooked 5. medium-rare
6. prefer 7. drink

Activity 3: Translation
1. 请问您有优惠券吗？
2. 今日的特价菜是什么？
3. 鲜炸鲈鱼是我们餐馆的招牌菜,您想尝尝吗？
4. 5杯果汁的价格相当于一扎果汁的价格。
5. 粉蒸肉只有我们餐厅才有。

Unit 15

Activity 1: Blank Filling
1. green crab 2. apologize 3. 15 minutes 4. have an appointment
5. 1920 6. room serve 7. on house 8. won't happen again

Activity 3: Translation

1. 能给我们拿一些牙签吗？
2. 我给您把大盘里的肉菜换到一个小盘里吧？
3. 出这房间往右拐，走几步就有一个免费公共电话。
4. 先生，上汤了，请您往边上挪一下？
5. 调料都在桌上，有醋、酱油、辣椒、蒜蓉、胡椒粉。

Unit 16

Activity 1: Blank Filling

1. room service 2. fresh orange juice 3. Three minutes 4. fresh milk
5. two three-minute eggs 6. boiled eggs 7. Room 1190

Activity 3: Translation

1. 这是我们餐厅的特色菜。
2. 酒单在菜单的最后一页。
3. 一共是550元，包括15%的服务费。
4. 您可以把这些东西放在门外的走廊里。
5. 我把餐布放在这里吧，这样您就可以面对电视看新闻了。

参考书目

Jonathan A. Hales. *Accounting and Financial Analysis in the Hospitality Industry*. Boston: Prentice Hall, 2011.

Raymond C. Ellis, Jr. and David M. Stipanuk. *Security and loss prevention management* (2nd ed.). Orlando: Educational Institute, American Hotel & Motel Association, 1999.

Raymond Cote. *Accounting for the Hospitality Industry* (5th ed.). Lansing: American Hotel & Lodging Educational Institute, 2007.

Raymond S. Schmidgall. *Hospitality Industry Managerial Accounting* (6th ed.). Lansing: Educational Institute, American Hotel & Motel Association, 2006.

Robert H. Woods, Misty M. Johanson, and Michael P. Sciarini. *Managing Hospitality Human Resources*. Lansing: American Hotel & Lodging, Educational Institute. 2012.

Rocco M. Angelo and Andrew N. Vladimir. *Hospitality Today: An Introduction* (7th ed.). Lansing: Educational Institute, American Hotel & Lodging Association, 2011.

陈丹:《酒店饭店英语口语实例大全》,北京:中国宇航出版社,2009。
陈文生:《酒店管理180个案例品析》,北京:中国旅游出版社,2007。
管燕红:《朗文现代酒店业英语》,北京:外语教学与研究出版社,2005。
胡朝慧:《酒店英语》,北京:北京大学出版社,2011。
浩瀚:《旅游酒店英语高频话题》,北京:中国水利水电出版社,2009。
姜玲:《房内用膳送餐员和康乐服务员岗位英语》,北京:旅游教育出版社,2007。
刘树荣:《酒店餐饮英语口语》,广州:广东省出版集团、广东经济出版社,2010。
刘海霞,张峥:《饭店英语360句》,北京:旅游教育出版社,2008年。
麦榕:《酒店英语》,北京:旅游教育出版社,2013。
王燕华、黄培希:《酒店英语》,北京:对外经济贸易大学出版社,2013。
肖璇,吴建华:《酒店基础英语口语教程》,北京:世界图书出版公司,2011。
谢朝刚,周名丁:《饭店对客服务指南》,北京:旅游教育出版社,2005。
张丽君:《酒店英语》,北京:清华大学出版社,2010。
周玮:《旅行社英语》,广州:广东旅游出版社,2005。

http://www.doc88.com/p-7912262 20231.html
http://www.housekeepingchannel.com/
http://www.good-housekeeping-magazine.com/
中国旅游教育网 www.tepcb.com
职业餐饮 http://www.canyin168.com/glyy/yg/ygpx/yypx/